For more information about the EBEA (Economics and Business Education Association) please telephone 01273 846033 or email: ebeah@pavilion.co.uk

BITESIZEbusiness studies

Introduction

About BITESIZE Business studies

BITESIZE Business studies is a revision guide that has been put together to help you with your GCSE exams. As the name tells you, the book is divided into bite-sized chunks, helping you to organize your revision into a task that is manageable. You can work your way steadily through the information given under each topic heading, and try the activities as you go. If you have videoed the linked BBC TV programmes, you can revise even more actively by watching them, and returning to their different sections as often as you need to. You can also gather more information on each topic by visiting the BBC Internet site.

BITESIZE Business studies forms a good solid structure to build your revision around, but of course cannot provide total coverage of all topics, or examples of every possible type of exam question. So you must also tie it in with your own notes taken from lessons and textbooks, and continue to ask your teachers for advice.

About this book

This book has six main sections, each of which is divided into smaller units and begins with an 'overview' page, telling you what will be covered in those units. Each section has features, such as **FactZONES**, which give key facts and terms to be learnt. Other recurring features are **practice questions**, showing the different types you might get in an exam, together with hints on how to answer them; and various different kinds of revision activity.

As you read through the book, take care to look out for any of the symbols shown on the left. The link symbol to the video shows that there is information to be found on the particular subject you are reading about, if you watch the video. It is a good idea, when you have found the linked material on the video, to take note of its position (jot down the time code in the margin of this book) so you can find it again. Words that appear in **bold type** are important ones to know the meaning of. They are defined near where they appear and you could collect them into a glossary for yourself.

If there are any areas that you are unsure about as you go through the book, you should go over your class notes again and ask your teacher for help. Don't be embarrassed about asking for help – most teachers are delighted to see students taking responsibility for their own learning. You could also contact the BITESIZE on-line team, who are there to help you.

GCSE Business studies exam questions

GCSE Business studies students are entered at one of two levels – Foundation or Higher Tier. There are examples of questions from both levels in this book.

THE ON-LINE SERVICE

You can find extra support, information and answers to your exam queries on the BITESIZE Internet site. The address is http://www.bbc.co.uk/education/revision

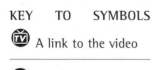

KEY TO SYMBOLS

📺 A link to the video

◎ An activity to do

❓ A question to think about

 # Business Studies

Editor: Paul Clarke

Authors: Sally Bates, David Cox, Dean Lithgoe, Jo Bentham, Paul Widdowson, Mark Tilling on behalf of the Economics and Business Education Association.

Published by BBC Educational Publishing, BBC White City,
201 Wood Lane, London W12 7TS
First published 1999 © EBEA, the Economics and Business Education Association/BBC Education, 1999
Reprinted 2000, Reprinted 2001 (twice)
ISBN: 0 563 46413 5
Printed in Great Britain by Bell & Bain Ltd., Glasgow

Contents

The questions vary from course to course, but most papers have some **short questions**, on particular topics, which require answers of one or two sentences or paragraphs (it will be clear from the style of question, and the space allowed in the answer booklet, how long your answer should be). Other questions are based on **case studies**, with source material to study. (This material, in some cases, is supplied before the exam.) These questions test your knowledge and understanding from right across the course, not just from one topic.

Case study questions are generally in two or three parts and the source material may include such things as photographs, drawings, newspaper cuttings, company information, tables or graphs. Typical first questions will ask about your understanding of this data (questions such as 'What do you understand by the term...'). Foundation Tier papers will normally just have two or three of this type of question.

Higher Tier papers generally have more extended case studies and problem-solving exercises, and questions are often 'open-ended', which means that there could be a range of possible answers. You are asked to evaluate or suggest solutions to business problems, and should list the points and data you would use to support your ideas. Typical questions include 'Why do you think the business chose to...', 'Explain the effect that this decision will have on...' and 'How can the firm improve its sales figures...'.

REMEMBER
There is usually more than one viewpoint on any problem. Make it clear, for example, if you are writing as a manager, a worker or a customer.

Understanding the questions

GCSE exams are not trying to catch you out. They aim to give you the opportunity to show what you know, in a clear, well-constructed way. So it's important that you read each question carefully and make sure you understand what it is asking you to do. Below are some words commonly used in business studies exam questions. Make sure you understand exactly what they mean.

Compare - identify and write down the similarities and differences between features stated in the question.

Define - write a definition of, meaning describe accurately or explain the meaning of.

Describe - write down details about what is shown in a resource such as a bar chart, newspaper report or graph.

Discuss (or **Analyse**) - usually requires a longer answer examining, describing and giving reasons. Also, maybe, explaining arguments for and against.

Explain (or **Account for**) - give reasons for a particular business decision or activity.

Give your views - say what you think or what another individual or group of people might think.

Identify - name, recognise or select a particular feature or features.

Name, state or **list** – write down accurate details or features.

Study – look carefully at a resource and think about what it shows.

With reference to (or **refer to**) **examples that you have studied** – when explaining the reasons for a particular answer, include details of specific case studies or other examples.

With the help of (or **using**) **the information provided** - include examples from the information on the exam paper to explain your answer.

Planning your revision

The secret of good revision is planning. Prepare a **revision timetable** three or four months before your exams, with time allotted to each of your subjects. Divide the days by the number of subjects, so you know how much time you've got for each. Then organize the time into batches – about three 40-minute sessions per day is enough for most people, and it is a good idea to keep to one subject per day.

Make sure you arrange it so that the subjects are evenly spread across the time available. Each subject should have some early batches of time allocated to basic learning and understanding, then some later sessions for self-testing and practice in answering questions.

Make sure your timetable includes short breaks between the sessions, and longer time-off slots, e.g. for sport or leisure. If you revise too hard for too long, you will not remember things very well.

R E M E M B E R
Give yourself a bit more time on subjects you're not that keen on. There's a great temptation to keep going over things you enjoy and know well!

What to revise

Your main revision aims should be to improve your **knowledge** and understanding of business ideas and behaviour, to improve your **recall** (your ability to 'unlock' this knowledge when it is needed) and also to learn how to **adapt** what you know, so that you can **apply** it to answering a wide range of questions. Below is a checklist to work from when going through your revision material. It will improve your level of marks in the exam if you have these basic elements covered:

■ key business terms

■ examples of good business case studies

■ information about, and explanations of, business decisions and business behaviour

■ causes and effect, e.g. impacts of technology or price changes on a business

■ similarities and differences between business organizations

■ attitudes and values of different interest groups

■ alternative views

■ advantages and disadvantages of different solutions to issues

How to revise

The best way to revise is to **do** something with the information you are trying to learn. If you **organize** it into short notes, lists, sketches, diagrams, flow charts, codes and tables, this will help you to learn it, and once in that form it is also easier to **memorize**. Try to bring together all your information from different sources in this way. You could use a highlighter pen to pinpoint key areas. Try making flash cards which summarize the points of a particular topic. Such cards can be made pocket-sized for carrying around and looking at in spare moments, such as on buses or trains.

Memorizing should always be based on: **look**, **cover**, **write**, **check**. As you go through this book, try working in this way. Close the book after reading each double page and write down the key facts it covered.

To revise well, you should read through your notes and lists on a regular basis, test your memory by checking and rechecking and, importantly, practise answering questions of different kinds. It is a good idea to get hold of some old exam papers - your teacher should be able to help you with this. You'll find that the same kind of question comes up year after year, so you can see the type of thing to expect.

On the day

At the start of the exam, remember to read and follow all the instructions on the front of each paper. If there is a choice of questions, read through each one carefully to make sure you choose the one(s) you know the most about. As you begin each question, read it again carefully so you understand what you're expected to do. It is a good idea to quickly plan out the longer answers, writing brief notes to remind yourself what to include.

Assess the time allowed overall, and the different lengths of the questions, to work out how much time to give to each. Some exam papers may say how many marks each question is worth, which gives you a clue as to how detailed each answer should be, and how long you should spend on it. Check your time during the exam and don't spend too long on one question. If a question is taking too long, leave it and move on to the next one. You should be able to make up time on questions that you find easier, so at the end of the exam there might be time to go back to the question you left unfinished.

If you haven't left enough time to answer a question properly, write down all your thoughts in an organized list of notes, to show the examiners how you would have approached the question and what you would have brought into the answer. This will get you some marks.

Write neatly and clearly and check your spelling, punctuation and grammar. Examiners cannot award marks to something they cannot read, and extra marks may be given for good English, particularly the correct spelling of specialist terms.

Good Luck!

! R E M E M B E R
Checking what you remember is an important part of revising. Try working with a friend, and testing each other.

7

Business types & objectives

This section is about:

- Sectors of business activity

- The different types of business

- Business organisation and internal structure

- Business objectives

Businesses can be classified (grouped together) and described in different ways.

For instance, if you want to look at which business activities are growing and which are declining, it is useful to look at them in terms of what product or service they produce, and therefore group them by sectors of activity or industrial groupings.

Alternatively, businesses can be classified by the way in which they are financed and controlled, or according to their different objectives.

Below you can see some examples of the range of business types that will be looked at in this section.

Types of business

John works on his own farm growing crops such as wheat. His family has farmed for generations. He is part of the primary sector (see opposite) supplying the big bread manufacturers.

Rank Hovis MacDougall plc is a large food manufacturer with many factories, and is run on behalf of shareholders. Their bread is sold in supermarkets all over the country. They like the quality of the product they buy from John's farm. They aim to provide affordable bread for customers and make good profits for the shareholders.

Co-Op supermarkets provide a wholesaling and retail service to get the bread and a wide range of other products to customers at a convenient site. They share the benefits of their business with their customers and workers, who are all part-owners.

Tom's bakery supplies high-quality bread and cakes to a local area. He shares the business with his partner. They get a lot of satisfaction from running their own business.

FactZONE

Sectors of business activity

Three major groupings are commonly used for classifying business activity:

Primary sector Businesses involved in getting raw materials from the land or sea.
Examples: farming, mining, fishing.

Secondary sector Businesses using raw materials to produce finished goods.
Examples: car manufacturers, clothing companies and makers of computers.

Tertiary sector Businesses providing a service to industry or to consumers.
Examples: banking, retail, call centres

Britain was once very dependent on the primary sector for income and jobs. Now the growing sector is the tertiary sector, as even manufacturing has been hit hard by competition from abroad.

Table: 1996 figures

sector	contribution to UK production	contribution to UK employment
primary sector	6%	2%
secondary sector	28%	28%
tertiary sector	66%	70%

Businesses in one sector are all linked to, and dependent on, those in other sectors, and at each stage in the chain a business will try to add value. A chain of production for the oil industry (as shown here on the right) demonstrates the interdependence of businesses.

Some businesses choose to link activities in one sector with those in another. This is called **vertical integration:**

1) An oil refining company might also become involved with extraction. This is known as **backward integration** because the business links backwards in the chain of production.
2) A take-over of petrol stations by an oil company would be described as **forward integration**.

When a business links with another in the same sector, it is called **horizontal integration**.

Business activity can also be classified in other ways, for instance into the **industrial groupings** shown below (used by the Government):

Agriculture, forestry and fishing
Energy and water
Manufacturing
Construction

Distribution, hotels, repairs
Transport and communication
Banking, finance and insurance
Education and health

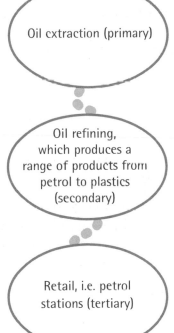

Oil extraction (primary)

Oil refining, which produces a range of products from petrol to plastics (secondary)

Retail, i.e. petrol stations (tertiary)

⊠ Different types of business

Businesses can be classified according to how they are owned and financed, and on the basis of their legal responsibilities.

You need to know:

■ how sole traders and partnerships are owned, managed and financed

■ the differences between private and public limited companies

■ the main features of co-operatives and franchises

■ how public sector companies differ from the private sector

Sole traders and partnerships

REMEMBER
Not everyone in business wants to run big companies. Sole traders enjoy the sense of being 'their own boss'.

Sole traders (**sole proprietors**) and **partnerships** are the smallest forms of business but are the easiest to set up. They make an important contribution to UK business activity (over 90% of businesses in the UK are either sole traders or partnerships). They carry big risks of failure and of incurring debts for their owners, but they also allow individuals to turn an enterprising idea or skill into a business activity.

> A sole trader is a business owned and controlled by one person. Sole traders operate under their own name and are responsible for the everyday running of the business. They are the most common type of business in the UK.

Partnerships are owned by the partners (there must be a minimum of two and usually a maximum of 20 partners). Responsibilities can be shared, and the business can draw on the different types of expertise of different partners. There is less disruption when someone leaves the business because other partners are still there to share their knowledge and keep contact with customers.

Most partnerships write a **Deed of Partnership** – a set of rules to follow if trust between partners breaks down. A Deed usually covers the sharing of profits and losses, the financial contribution of each partner, their responsibilities, and how partners may be added to or removed from the business. Under the 1980 Partnership Act, everything is shared equally if there is no such Deed or similar formal agreement.

Whether sole trader or partnership, the basics for setting up in business are:
■ permission to trade in an area (a local council licence may be needed)
■ registration to pay VAT (Value Added Tax) if the turnover of the business is above a certain level
■ profit and loss accounts and a balance sheet so that the business can be assessed for tax and insurance contributions
■ a knowledge of health and safety laws and a willingness to obey the rules.

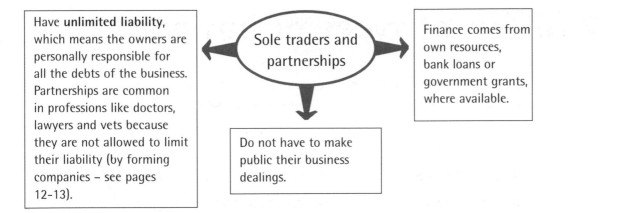

Have **unlimited liability**, which means the owners are personally responsible for all the debts of the business. Partnerships are common in professions like doctors, lawyers and vets because they are not allowed to limit their liability (by forming companies – see pages 12-13).

Sole traders and partnerships

Finance comes from own resources, bank loans or government grants, where available.

Do not have to make public their business dealings.

Advantages and disadvantages

Sole trader	
✓	makes all the decisions, keeps all the profits, has total control, small start up costs, can keep the business flexible, lots of job satisfaction
✗	unlimited liability (can lose personal wealth if business fails), lack of capital (so can't bulk buy, do market research etc), pressure of responsibility

Partnership	
✓	easy to set up, lots of expertise available through partners, more finance available than to the trader, shared responsibilities mean less pressure
✗	liability still rests with partners, each partner is responsible for debts of others, disagreements possible

Practice question

John Taylor opened his newsagency as a sole trader in 1991 with the help of his wife. He had previously worked for a big chain of stores and now wanted a new challenge. It cost him £5000 to set up and he was then left to work long hours when his wife became ill. He employed an assistant manager but the shop started to lose money. The shelves were half empty and customers complained that there were never enough daily papers. John decided to go into partnership with a friend.

1. Using examples drawn from the case study above or from your own knowledge, explain the meaning of the following:

   a) unlimited liability
   b) partnership

2. a) Describe three advantages of being a sole trader.
   b) What reasons might explain why one third of sole traders go out of business within their first year of operation?

❓ *For question 1, think about explaining the terms, but also use the given example (or one of your own) to be more specific. What do the terms mean to John Taylor? Question 2 needs good knowledge of advantages and disadvantages. It requires slightly longer answers, and would carry more marks.*

Private and public limited companies

Companies are different from sole traders and partnerships, both in the way they are run and financed, and in the risks they pose to their owners. They may be locally based with a modest turnover or a multinational giant with millions of shareholders and production or retail activities in many different countries. The turnover of some multinational companies is larger than the income of some countries.

There are two types of company - **private limited companies (Ltds)** and **public limited companies (plcs)**. Both types raise finance by selling shares to people. These **shareholders** are the owners of the company; they have a say in the running of the company and share in its profits (by way of annual **dividends** paid to them), but the company has its own legal identity, separate from that of the shareholders.

The 'limited' in both cases refers to **limited liability**. While the size of their share decides how much profit shareholders gain, it also limits their risk of losses - they only stand to lose the money they have invested in the business.

12

Ltd

A private limited company (Ltd) is usually a small to medium-sized business.
- It sells shares privately to family or friends
- The original owners, as the board of directors, keep control. Managers are usually appointed to run the day-to-day business.
- Private limited companies find it comparatively hard to raise finance from banks for expansions, etc.

⊚ *Look up share prices in the financial pages of the larger newspapers or on the BBC news website. Find examples of companies (plcs) which have high share prices and which are moving up or down over the week/month. List some of these companies to use as examples in your exam.*

Plc

A public limited company (plc) is usually a much larger company.
- It sells shares to the general public through the Stock Exchange in London.
- The original owners often lose control over decision-making, as it is the shareholders who appoint the board of directors to oversee the business, and employ managers. The interests of shareholders and managers may be different - because of this, the AGM and annual report are important in keeping everyone informed and involved.
- Public limited companies find it easier to raise additional finance to help fund further developments in the business. Banks and financial institutions are willing to buy shares and lend money more readily than they would to a Ltd.

It is generally a similar process to set up both a Ltd and a plc, but there are more rules and regulations for a plc. Company information and rules are sent to the official registrar of companies, who grant a Certificate of Incorporation. Shares are sold and the company starts trading. In the case of a plc, there has to be at least £50 000 of finance available and a prospectus of financial detail drawn up for possible shareholders.

Limited liability means no-one is personally liable for company debts.

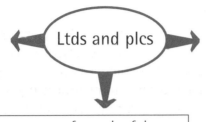

Ltds and plcs

Have to have an Annual General Meeting (AGM) and produce an annual report for shareholders. Also must have audited accounts, which are sent to the registrar of companies and are then open to public scrutiny.

Finance comes from sale of shares, bank loans, government grants where available.

Main differences between Ltds and plcs

Ltds	Plcs
shares sold only to founders, relatives and friends	shares listed on Stock Exchange, sold to public
at least 1 shareholder, 1 director, 1 secretary	at least 2 shareholders, 2 directors, qualified Company Secretary
takes time to sell shares no minimum capital	shares sold easily minimum share capital £50 000
founders of company retain control	original owners may have little influence on decisions
less status than plc,; loans more difficult	large organisation, high status, good credit rating
shareholders likely to agree on objectives	may be divisions between shareholders and managers

Practice question

Greens Ltd sells a range of nuts and crisps to the general public and to the catering trade.

Shares are owned by a small group of the Green family.

1 a) What do the letters Ltd stand for?

   b) Identify two important features of a Ltd.

   c) The owners of *Greens* have limited liability. What does this mean?

d) Why might the Green family be unwilling to turn the company into a plc, even though they badly need the finance they would raise by issuing new shares?

(?) *The first three parts need short accurate answers with definitions. In part b), you should say **why** the feature is important. In part d) you need to explain what the family would see as disadvantages.*

Co-operatives

Co-operatives are businesses run by a group of people with a shared interest in the business, for the benefit of all involved. Each participant has an equal say. These 'caring and sharing' features and objectives of the business are the crucial difference between co-operatives and other types of business.

The most common type of co-operative is a **workers' co-operative**, where workers buy or set up the business and then share decision-making and profits equally.

In worker co-operatives, each worker puts in an equal amount of money. This has often been redundancy money in the UK as workers have chosen to buy out their firm rather than accept unemployment.

✓	Usually good industrial relations.
✓	Workers are well-motivated.
✓	The business has close ties with the people of the local area.
✗	There may be few chances of successful expansion – banks often lack confidence in co-ops, so are reluctant to loan money.
✗	Decision-making can be difficult.
✗	The best workers may want more reward than others.
✗	There may be limited business experience among the workers, but an unwillingness to buy manager expertise.

A **producer co-operative** is a group of producers who set up their own marketing and retail operation, to reduce costs and offer lower prices to consumers.

Producer co-operatives can be found amongst farmers and wine-growers. Expensive machinery can be bought and shared, and products are sold directly to consumers from the site, or from wholesale premises. Café Direct is an example. It markets coffee in a way which gives a fair price for coffee growers and ensures better working conditions.

A **consumer co-operative** is set up by a group of consumers to buy goods in bulk and share any resulting profits.

The best known UK co-op is the group including the Co-op Retail Society and the Co-op Bank. The retail movement (consumer co-operative) set up in Rochdale, Lancashire, in the 1840s now has over 5000 shops nationwide and a turnover of over £8 million.

The Rochdale Co-op used principles which have guided other consumer co-ops:
- each members has one vote,
- anyone can buy a share,
- goods and services are sold at a reasonable price with profits returned to members in proportion to the amount they have spent.

! R E M E M B E R
Co-operatives are important because they offer a different way of running a business.

Franchises

A **franchise** allows a small trader (sole trader, partnership or company, known as the franchisee) to use a well-known company's trade name, image and products in return for regular fees, and allows the well-known large firm to operate in many different places using the experience of local managers.

- McDonalds, The Body Shop and Holiday Inn are some well-known examples. In 1994, there were over 19 000 franchises in the UK.

- Franchises have a better success rate than sole traders as a way of starting a business from scratch, but there can be difficulties agreeing on the amount of control franchise holders have over day-to-day decisions.

Advantages to franchiser

Business grows without risk of debt (franchisee responsible for debts)

Regular income

Less organisation and staff than if a branch were opened

Keep control (including the choice of franchisee in the first place)

Franchisees are usually well-motivated people with local knowledge

Advantages to franchisee

Less risk during start-up

Keep most of the profits (sometimes a percentage of income is paid to franchiser)

Selling established product

Using successful brand image

Help and training available

There is national marketing at less expense

◎ *List, in order of importance, the advantages to you as a franchisee if you were starting up in business as:*

a) a fruit-seller on a market stall

b) a fast-food restaurant

c) a mobile-phone shop

Practice question

Mike and Alan enjoy skateboarding and are good at making boards. They decided to set up a business using a rented workshop underneath the railway arches in Manchester. They pooled their money and bought some materials. Neither liked the task of marketing and selling the boards, though. At the end of six months, they had only sold a couple to friends, were still paying rent, and had no storage room left.

1) What advantages would there be in buying a franchise from a national skateboarding and leisure company?

2) What extra costs would have to be paid if Mike and Alan bought a franchise?

(?) *What could a national chain offer to Mike and Alan? Think about what the franchiser will expect in return.*

The public sector

Some big organisations are so important to a nation that the government chooses to own and control them. They are financed by taxes as well as by selling goods and services, and are collectively described as **public sector** organisations. They are directly responsible to either the national or local government.

Governments regard these organisations as important for a variety of different reasons:

■ **security reasons**
The activities of some organisations are seen as vital to the defence of a nation, and to its internal stability. It would be dangerous to have private armies or police forces. Others may be thought of as 'politically sensitive' (e.g. arms research, disposal of nuclear waste).

■ **economic reasons**
Some areas of activity are essential to the economy, such as the coal industry, or are seen as natural monopolies which might be tempted to exploit customers (railways, gas).

■ **financial reasons**
The capital investment required for equipment in some cases could not be borne by a private company (railways, power stations).

■ **social reasons**
Some organisations provide essential services (emergency services, education, health service) and work for the public benefit (Post Office, BBC). Access to these must be ensured for all levels of society.

REMEMBER
Do not mix up the public sector (government-owned) with public limited companies (plcs — privately owned, but with shares available to the public).

Co-ordinating agencies are another type of organisation included in the public sector. They are set up to co-ordinate activities of private businesses (e.g. English Nature, Training and Enterprise Councils) or to ensure that businesses follow rules to protect consumers (Trading Standards Authority).

◎ *The Post Office provides a range of services, from an international mail service and national bank (Giro), to welfare and pension payments at small local post offices. Make a list of what disadvantages and advantages there might be if the Post Office were run purely for profit.*

Some industries (e.g. water, electricity, railways) were **nationalised** (taken into the public sector) by governments in the past because it was thought to be more efficient to co-ordinate one national network rather than to have competing businesses.

In the UK, before 1979, the government owned well over fifty of the country's largest business organisations.

From 1979, the Conservative government began **privatising** many industries (e.g. BT, British Gas, British Petroleum, British Airways, British Rail) - they returned them to the private sector by selling shares to private businesses and ordinary people.

They believed that managers and workers would operate more efficiently if motivated by competition and profit, that the public would gain from share dividends, and that government could still use tight regulations to keep a measure of control.

Some reasons given For...		...and Against privatisation
✔	Control in private hands.	✗ Many of these industries are monopolies and can charge high prices or cut services.
✔	More people can be share owners.	✗ Private industry is not interested in providing non-profitable services that bring social benefits.
✔	More competition encourages efficiency.	✗ Private industry may not afford key investment.
✔	Reduces the need for government subsidies.	✗ Competition can be wasteful as resources are duplicated.
✔	Private sector is better and quicker at making decisions.	✗ Profits go to the wealthy who can afford shares.
		✗ There may be a risk of job losses.

Public and private sector mixes

In some public sector industries, competition was introduced in different ways.
Internal markets: in the health service and local council services, departments have to compete against each other (and sometimes against private companies) to win contracts. Schools have been given control over their own budgets and some compete for pupils in local areas.
Private finance: since 1992, businesses bidding to build schools, hospitals and roads have been expected to provide more of the finance.
Quangos: Quasi Autonomous Non-Governmental Organisations are partly independent but are government-funded. They include the British Tourist Board, the Environmental Agency and National Parks.

Practice question

1) What is meant by privatisation?
2) What effects can privatisation have on:
   a) the objectives of an industry?
   b) the quality of the goods and services it provides?
   c) competition and the price of its products

Think of an example, such as British Telecom and try to base your answer around it. What difference has it made to BT now the company has shareholders and customers to please and competitors to face? How might the changes in the way it is financed suit its needs?

Business organisation

All businesses need to be organised. Some are simple organisations where responsibilities and communication are easy. Larger businesses are more complicated; they may have many different departments and sites with thousands of employees. They need very clear channels of communication and lines of responsibility.

You need to know:

■ the differences in organisation between small and large businesses

■ how an organisation chart is drawn up

A small business, such as a local newsagents, may have an owner and an assistant. Responsibility for big decisions is with the owner and although the assistant has a formal work contract, most communications can be direct, verbal and informal. They can also be informal, for example, in a small partnership, where there is just one level, with all partners having an equal say in decisions.

Larger businesses, employing more staff, need a structure and more formal ways of communicating. Some may set out to be very democratic and share responsibilities and decisions with as many people as possible. They may have an internal structure based on groups with common interests, or on friendship groups. Others (most) have a different, **hierarchical**, culture, with a tradition of handing down decisions to the many, from the few at the top.

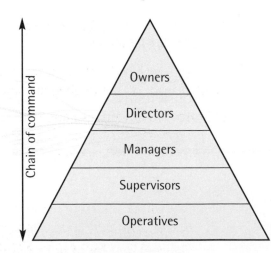

The **chain of command** is very clear in such a business: at each level, people with different roles and responsibilities take orders and instructions from above and give them to those below. They send requests and complaints upwards. The communications system reflects the formal business culture, with lots of written notices and memos, formal reports, and meetings with written agendas and detailed minutes. It is thorough and detailed but may be expensive and time-consuming.

How a business divides up into units can vary. The most common forms are:
■ by function (based on the jobs people do)
■ by product (separate department for each product made)
■ by geographical area (local branches, or national divisions etc)

(For more about communication at work, see pages 58-60.)

A typical **organisation chart**, showing a business divided up by function:

Board of directors
(reporting to shareholders)

Managing director

Finance Manager — Human Resources Manager — Production Manager — Marketing Manager — Logistics Manager

Staff Staff — Staff Staff — Staff Staff — Staff Staff — Staff Staff

Chain of command

Span of control
(of managing director). The term means the number
of people over whom a person has direct authority

A business with too long a chain of command, or with spans of control that are too wide, may find decisions are hard to take and rules hard to enforce. **Delegation** is a common and efficient way of solving such problems. Authority for particular areas or tasks is passed down to a lower level.

◎ *Draw an organisation chart for your school or college. Think about the separate responsibilities for teaching (curriculum) and pastoral work (form tutors, year heads etc). What differences are there in the span of control of the Head of the English Department and of the teacher in charge of IT?*

Practice question

The directors of *Tolworth* have re-organised their business; Jack Davison will be chairman, Paul Singh finance manager, Daniel Davison retail manager, Chris Davison production manager and Francesca Davison managing director.

1) From the information above, draw this part of the organisation chart.

2) The organisation chart shows a division of labour within the company. Explain the term division of labour.

3) List three business functions of an organisation other than finance and production.

4) Explain the terms 'chain of command' and 'span of control'.

5) State two job roles within the span of control of the finance manager.

6) State two advantages and two disadvantages of a hierarchy as a form of business organisation.

❓ *Think how you can answer these short questions briefly. Your answers must be to the point. Your explanations in parts 2 and 4 should outline the main ideas and give examples of how they work in a business, and remember in part 6 to say* **why** *things are advantages or disadvantages.*

Business objectives

The stated **objectives** (aims) of a business show why it is following a particular course or strategy. A business will decide its general objectives, and then use these to set more detailed targets. The success of the business can then be measured by looking at whether these targets have been reached. Business objectives can be found in company reports, in publicity materials and in posters displayed in their buildings. A set of objectives provides a statement of purpose for the business and it is often referred to as a **mission statement**.

You need to know:

■ the similarities and differences in the objectives of private and public sector businesses

■ what kinds of targets businesses set for themselves

■ the different objectives of different stakeholders

There are three basic types of objective, depending on the type of business organisation:

(1) To make a profit – the key concern for most private businesses from sole traders to large companies.

(2) To provide a service and break even - most public sector businesses are set up to provide a service. Schools, hospitals and leisure centres are often run by local councils to provide a service to the community. They are usually expected just to cover their costs.

(3) To be charitable – some businesses are set up solely to help others. They operate as any efficient business and often have to compete for funds.

Within these general headings, businesses set themselves more detailed objectives. Examples of these, and ways they might be achieved, are shown below.

■ to maximise profits, by charging the highest possible prices
■ to win a larger share of the market, by taking over a rival business
■ to plan for long term survival, by borrowing money to invest in developing new products
■ to ensure services reach those in most need, by restricting them to a named group at a time
■ to keep and strengthen independence and flexibility by setting up a new branch

Once taken up as policy, these objectives are documented in much finer detail, and targets are set (e.g. a certain increase in profit by a certain date). To be of use when measuring success, these targets need to be **SMART:**

S pecific
M easurable
A ttainable
R ealistic
T imed

Some objectives are measurable and short term, like profit; others are more general and long term, such as independence and survival. Also, different businesses give their objectives different levels of importance.

A balance is always needed. The main objective of most private businesses is profit, but it will not always be profit at any price. Some businesses are keen to provide customer satisfaction and to keep up a reputation for quality. They may accept a drop in profits or sales to keep their independence.

Public sector businesses aim to provide a good service, with high levels of customer satisfaction, fast speed of response and efficient use of resources, but they must balance these things against working to tight financial targets.

❗ REMEMBER

Some objectives and targets may be shared by really quite different businesses.

❓ *Think about the businesses in your nearest shopping centre. Are the objectives of large and small shops the same? What are likely to be the objectives of a shop managed by a charity, and a small independent greengrocer?*

Stakeholders are the people who have an interest in the success of a business. Their objectives are often different:

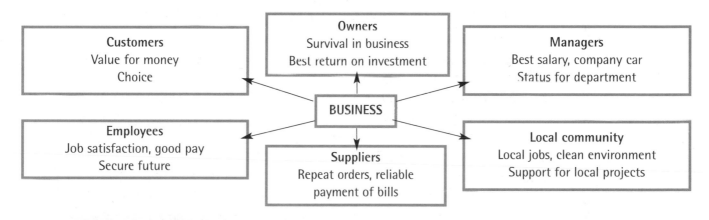

Customers	Owners	Managers
Value for money, Choice	Survival in business, Best return on investment	Best salary, company car, Status for department

BUSINESS

Employees	Suppliers	Local community
Job satisfaction, good pay, Secure future	Repeat orders, reliable payment of bills	Local jobs, clean environment, Support for local projects

Practice question

A clothes manufacturer, *Ragbags Ltd.*, makes and sells children's clothes in the North of England. The managers want to increase sales in the South, where they would need to open several new stores. Some shareholders are worried that the new investment will affect the profitability of the company.

1. Why might the managers want to increase sales?
2. Why might some shareholders be more interested in keeping profits high?
3. How might expansion affect customers?

4. What might the managers say that would persuade shareholders to support the expansion?

❓ *Different stakeholders might appear to have different views, but perhaps shareholders can be persuaded that the investment will mean more profits to share in the longer term. Examiners would want you to show that stakeholders can have some shared and some conflicting interests.*

Business production

This section is about:

- Product choice and scale of production

- Methods of production

- Efficiency and new technology

- Quality management

- Business location

How do businesses decide what goods to make and on what scale to make them? In the past, businesses tended to make products first, and then think about selling them at a later point. Now, most businesses are market-orientated (see pages 66-67). Customer preferences are researched and products are identified that will satisfy these preferences and needs. A business then tries to make the products in a way which keeps costs below the price customers would be willing to pay. This may mean finding new production methods and using large-scale processes.

Product and means of production

Research suggests parents are willing to pay up to £8 for a well-printed, colourful and well-written children's fiction book. A publishing company is set up, with the intention of producing a range of books for different markets, of which the children's section is one.

High-quality illustrations are commissioned from an artist and a top writer completes the story. A design team uses desk-top publishing technology to draw all the elements together and prepare the book for publishing. This is expensive work as each person's contribution is highly skilled.

At the printer's, thousands of copies are printed using new technology. Firms with good quality control make sure problems are sorted out at an early stage. A firm may relocate its printing business, to keep costs down or make use of better facilities. They may also receive a government grant for doing so.

Distributors use warehouses to store the books, and large trucks to move them to high street retailers. A warehouse located in the centre of the area of distribution helps to keep transport costs down.

FactZONE

Product choice

Businesses can be categorised according to their product base:

- **Sole product** businesses. Rely on just one product, for instance a farmer raising beef cattle. This is good if the product is a quality one which is hard to obtain, but can be risky as there is nothing to fall back on if demand for the product suddenly falls.
- Businesses with a wide **product range**. For instance, a large motor company making family cars, luxury cars, business vans, tractors, etc. Customers have greater choice and the business spreads its risks. Can be difficult to manage on a large scale while keeping down costs.
- Business with a wide **product mix**. For instance a company making food products, cleaning products, wrapping materials, etc. Risks are spread across different products in different markets. It can be difficult to manage products which are outside the business's 'core activity'.

Businesses need ways of assessing the performance of their products. The **'Boston Matrix'**, or **'Boston Box'** (see below) is a model which provides a framework for assessing sales growth and market share:

	High	Market share	Low
Fast	☆ **'Stars'** Likely to give good cash returns; need a lot of advertising.		? **'Question Marks'** Difficult to be sure of their future; need lots of investment.
Market growth			
Slow	🐄 **'Cash Cows'** Steady market; well-set products which can be 'milked' for profits.		🐕 **'Dogs'** Poor market share; need to be killed off.

Scale of production

Small firms, producing goods on a small scale, have high unit costs but can offer:
- personal service
- flexibility in meeting different demands
- specialist products
- mainly local service

Larger firms can take advantage of economies of scale - reductions in unit costs when producing larger quantities. Economies of scale may be:

- *technical economies* - large firms can use machinery more effectively (a 10 ton truck does not cost twice as much to run as a 5 ton truck).
- *trading economies* - large firms can buy in bulk at favourable prices.
- *financial economies* - large firms can usually borrow more at lower interest rates.
- *managerial economies* - large firms can hire specialist highly-skilled management.

There is a point at which firms may become too large to manage efficiently, and costs begin to rise again. For example, a firm with many factories in different parts of the country may develop communications problems, leading to inefficiency and increased costs.

Methods of production

Businesses use research to determine the best methods of production for their type of business, and monitor these production methods closely for any changes which could be made to improve efficiency. Businesses that depend on each other for supplies and orders can be tied even more closely together by their production methods.

You need to know:

■ the differences between job, batch and flow production methods

■ the advantages and disadvantages of different methods of production

Most businesses use a mix of production methods but classifying them separately helps to identify the main features and advantages of each.

■ **Job production**: The production of a unique item from start to finish, e.g. a house extension, a ship or a road bridge, in response to an individual order.

■ **Batch production**: Larger-scale production of 'batches' of similar items, e.g. sweets, bread, clothing. An entire batch of products is processed through a production stage before moving on to the next stage. Machinery is reset at the earlier stage, and a new batch of different items is then processed. Production is aimed at the market rather than the individual customer.

■ **Flow** (or **mass**) **production**: Continuous production of identical items, e.g. newspapers, glass bottles, cars. The items flow through a set of specialised operations on an assembly line. Division of labour is essential, with workers trained to do specialist tasks. Production is aimed at the largest markets of all.

❗ REMEMBER

Businesses often combine different methods of production when making a range of products.

	Advantages	Disadvantages
Job production	High quality product made by skilled workers. Job satisfaction high. Easy to isolate problem areas.	Expensive materials. Expensive labour. Slow process, machinery often idle. Repeat orders unlikely.
Batch production	Lower unit costs (increased scale of production). Flexibility possible in batch quantity, according to demand. More specialised machinery with less idle time.	Costly storage needed. Some repetition in jobs. Batches need to be moved. Machinery needs re-setting.
Flow production	Large output, low unit cost. Good use of production time. Low-skilled, easily-trained labour. Products of standard quality.	Large investment in machinery. Inflexible assembly line. Repetitive work, poor motivation. Products all the same. Breakdowns cause big problems.

Just-in-Time (JIT) production

JIT production (also known as **lean production**) is a relatively new development, whereby stocks of raw materials, parts and components are made available in just the right quantity at the right time. Each separate load arrives at the factory's assembly line, fully quality-checked, just in time for it to be used in the production process.

JIT needs very careful management and close ties with suppliers (computer-controlled information links are a vital part of the process), but it can save large amounts of time and money that would otherwise be spent on storage and internal stock movement. Breakdowns in the system can cause costly delays, though.

Teamwork

In all production processes, teamwork is essential. In larger scale batch or flow production, teams of workers are typically responsible for one section or cell of the process, and control speed, quality and problem-spotting. Greater job-satisfaction can be gained if they are trained in the right way.

Some computer-controlled processes have led to less teamwork and more part-time work, with less job security and satisfaction.

◎ *You manage a local radio station playing new CD tracks and running lots of competitions with prizes. You are about to meet a supplier who promises to meet all your needs on a 'just in time' basis. Write down the main points you would want to put in a contract with the supplier.*

Practice question

Crown Fashions Ltd make clothes for major high street stores. The stores require a range of sizes, colours and designs for each garment. To meet these requirements, *Crown* uses batch production methods.

1. What is batch production?

2. Why are batch production methods particularly suited to the manufacture of clothing?

❓ *Think about why the other methods of production would not be appropriate. This will help you spot reasons for batch production. You need to write a clear and simple definition, followed by an application to the example given in the question.*

Efficiency and new technology

A business needs to be efficient in order to compete successfully. Efficiency can be increased by innovation and the use of new technology in the production process.

You need to know:

■ the meaning of efficiency and how it can be measured

■ examples of new technology used in manufacture

■ the benefits and costs of technological change

❗ REMEMBER

New technology can lead to job redundancies but it can also lead to lower prices, more demand and new jobs.

Most businesses judge efficiency on the basis of maximum output at the least possible cost. With a product such as a tin of beans, it is easy to measure the number produced by a worker or machine in a certain time. Improvements can come from the greater automation (greater use of machinery), from changing work practices and from productivity deals with workers. Businesses may also use unit costs as a measure. Falling unit costs is a good sign of improving efficiency.

Computer-controlled technology at a whole factory level, or for a very specific task, has made big improvements in some industries (e.g. car production). There is often better quality and control though the initial expense is high and workers may be made redundant.

Practice question

Read the FactZONE opposite, but then cover it before you try this question.

Berrywood Garden Centre employs four production staff and three in sales. Ten part-timers are also employed, some on a seasonal basis. The centre is planning to expand and to introduce automation, CAM and computer control systems into the hothouses where the plants are grown. This would make it more capital-intensive.

1. State the meaning of:
   a) automation   b) CAM
   c) computer control systems

2. How could these new technologies be used in the hothouses?

3. Explain the meaning of the term capital-intensive.

4. Explain how the introduction of new technology might affect the work of *Berrywood* employees.

❓ *Think about producing short, simple answers for this style of question. Part 1 wants simple definitions, while part 2 is looking for application of the ideas to the business setting. Part 3 needs a definition and an example of what it means for Berrywood. For part 4, you could think of a possible short-term and a long-term effect.*

FactZONE

Measures of efficiency used by businesses

- Productivity (e.g. output per team, per person, per man-hour, per machine)

- Unit costs (= total costs divided by quantity produced)
  Rising unit costs suggest production costs have gone up or the quantity of goods made has fallen.

- Idle resources (e.g. machines and workers standing idle)
  Usually found by observation and work-studies. Can be improved by changing work-practices, by mechanisation, by use of part-time workers.

- Stock levels
  Too few stocks and production may be stopped; too many stocks can lead to a firm being left with old goods that no one wants.

- Product quality (e.g. lots of goods returned to business with complaints)

- Poor management (e.g. evidence of many inefficiencies right across factory)
  A firm may need to invest in management training or re-organisation.

New Technology

CAM (computer-aided manufacturing)
In processes such as engineering, computers programme machines to complete work to a degree of accuracy which would be beyond a human. Provided the expensive machines (robots) are well-maintained, they continue to work with consistency in any conditions for 24 hours a day. Robots are ideal for dangerous, dirty or heavy jobs, too.

CAD (computer-aided design)
Products can now be designed on screen. Computer software can create 3-dimensional models with complex calculations. Production processes can be planned in advance, saving expensive research time and avoiding costly mistakes.

CIM (computer-integrated manufacturing)
CIM factories combine all the latest technological developments so that everything is controlled by computers. Computer control systems take a lot of investment but can cut labour costs by 80-90%. The computer programming team replaces the old factory managers. Products can be made on a large scale but 'custom-made' in assembly to meet individual customer needs.

Costs of new technology

- High investment costs can make it a risk.
- The firm needs to make large quantities to make a profit.
- New developments may make machines/software quickly out-of-date.
- Some workers are 'de-skilled' and redundant.
- Some workers find less job satisfaction in working with computer-controlled processes.

Quality management

Businesses have to decide where to pitch the quality of their product. Sometimes, as with clothes, design and appearance may be more important than quality. Traditional methods of quality control have relied on sample checks; new methods try to shift responsibility for quality to all employees.

You need to know:

■ the meaning of 'quality management'

■ examples of traditional and modern methods of quality management

The quality of a product can be set:

by law

Some products, e.g. car safety belts and drug products, have to undergo research checks. They must meet set standards and pass tests before they are allowed to be sold. National standards are checked and enforced by government.

by customer expectations

Businesses look to maintain quality in response to customer feedback ('we buy these because they last longer').

by the firm itself

Businesses are competitive with regard to rival producers (e.g. aiming to be the best value within a given price range).

 REMEMBER

Customers often put quality before price when choosing a product.

A business has to decide who will be responsible for quality and how the organisation can ensure quality at a reasonable cost.

Traditionally, the **quality control department** has been seen as 'responsible' for all matters relating to improving and maintaining the quality of the product (such things as monitoring machine performance, checking the quality of bought-in supplies, analysing the best use of manpower and possible improvements in design, etc.).

Increasingly, though, firms are introducing ideas of **TQM (total quality management)**, whereby all staff are involved in an overall 'quality policy' aimed at 'zero defects' and targeted at the customer.

A new, modern style of quality management process cannot be just 'stuck on' to an old-fashioned system. Good teamwork is required and businesses with 'quality circles' (voluntary groups meeting often to discuss ways of improving work and production) find the move to total quality management much easier than those without.

Quality management

Traditional methods

Post-production quality control, where a quality controller or control team randomly checks finished goods for defects, etc. This is a wasteful procedure, as faults are only found at the end.
A slight improvement on this method is process control, where the controller or team samples products throughout the process of production.

Modern methods

TQM involves everyone in the process, improving the motivation of all staff. Faults are spotted and sorted out quickly.
Costs are involved, though, as workers need to be educated and trained to measure and monitor quality and seek improvement.
Kaizen - a Japanese idea of continual improvement is the ultimate interpretation of TQM. Workers are encouraged to suggest improvements as often as possible, with the result that possible concerns are dealt with before they turn into problems.

A top quality process should not only lead to good quality products but allow workers to operate safely and should protect the environment and cut down waste. Some businesses are currently trying out 'cradle to grave' environmental audits through which they check their processes for pollution, and try to recycle materials and cut the use of non-renewable resources wherever possible.

◎ *As part of your business studies, you could visit a biscuit factory which uses total quality management. List the things you might see that would confirm this quality system is working well.*

Practice question

GRC employs seventy workers at its main factory making plastic moulded products for kitchens. All their products are made from plastic granules, which are melted and put into moulds. This process is computer controlled. On the other side of town, GRC has a smaller factory with a supervisor and six people employed in assembly and packaging.

1. GRC is considering moving assembly and packaging on to the main site. Do you think this is a good idea? Give reasons.

2. The production manager believes everyone needs to be involved in quality control.

a) What is meant by 'quality control'?

b) Describe ways in which GRC might try to obtain a high standard of quality control.

⁇ *Think about savings that might be made. The case study doesn't give much detail, so when you make assumptions in your answer (about the factory or production methods), make it clear that you are doing so. In part 2, make sure you give a definition and also an example related to GRC.*

Business location

In choosing its location, a business has many factors to consider, both economic (such as keeping labour costs low) and non-economic (complying with government legislation). Some of these may conflict, but the best solution is one that correctly balances the relative importance of all the different factors.

You need to know:

■ the main factors that influence the location of businesses

■ the sources of help available to business

Factors affecting business location

Labour
A business needing a highly skilled workforce needs to be in an area linked to the industry, or one with local training facilities. A business looking for mainly unskilled, cheap labour looks for an area with a plentiful supply. Locating elsewhere might mean costs in transporting staff, or persuading them to relocate.

Raw materials and the market
Firms dealing with perishable goods, such as canning and freezing firms, need to be near to where the goods are produced. Businesses whose process is bulk-reducing, e.g. a brickmakers or a sawmill, also try to locate near to the source of materials, so they will have lower overall transport costs (materials in, then goods out to market). Bulk-increasing businesses, such as car manufacturers, do the opposite and try to be close to the market.

Other influences
Climate, competition and/or co-operation with other businesses and government/pressure group influence, may all play a role in location choice.

Land
The amount and cost of land clearly affect a business's choice of location, but so do things such as the nature of the land. Oil refineries and chemical plants need large, flat sites, which can bear heavy loads. A site in bad condition needs more money spent on it, and local planning restrictions must also be considered.

Infrastructure and services
All businesses need good sources of energy and water, efficient drainage and waste disposal, and good communications. Locating to a remote, undeveloped site means paying to link up to such systems. Being close to fast, efficient transport links is also vital.

Government and pressure groups

Increasingly, central and local government, and the influence of private pressure groups, play an important role in both encouraging and discouraging businesses to locate in certain areas.

The UK and European Governments provide financial support (such as tax-free grants and subsidies) to businesses willing to move to areas of high unemployment, and 24 Enterprise zones have been set up in the UK. (See page 85.)

Recent government policy has encouraged businesses to move to 'greenfield' sites - old farm or wasteland where new, purpose-built industrial estates have been created - or to 'brownfield' sites - derelict industrial areas in the heart of cities.

In other areas, the government has powers to restrict land use (e.g. the size of a proposed development) or disallow it altogether.

Business must also take note of pressure groups, which may try to discourage development for environmental or safety reasons, such as pollution and the protection of habitats, or the siting of dangerous activities (e.g. the processing of toxic waste) too close to human populations.

REMEMBER

The reasons for location may be unique to a business or its owner.

A very profitable business which reprocesses dangerous chemicals wants to locate in a run-down industrial area outside a large town. Can you think what arguments for and against the development might be put to a planning meeting?

Practice question

Monsterworld is one of three theme parks run by *Leisure plc* and has proved profitable since it opened. It is in a sunny climate on the coast where visitors are used to going and is well supplied by hotels. The transport infrastructure (roads, rail and air links) have all been praised.

1. Give three factors that a business should consider in locating a theme park.

2. Place in order of importance the factors which you have chosen. Explain the reasons for your chosen order.

Think about location factors relevant to the leisure industry. You might want to refer to factors not mentioned in the extract. For part 2, there is no right order. It is up to you to explain your own ideas, but make clear any assumptions you make about the business or the area.

Business finance

This section is about:

- Financial planning

- Covering costs and breaking even

- Cash flow and cash flow forecasting

- Drawing up financial statements

- Measuring financial performance

Finance (money) is the lifeblood of any organisation – without it, a firm cannot operate. Either it will not be able to get started or it will find it difficult to carry on trading. Bills have to be paid and employees want their wages.

Many firms with successful product ideas go under because of poor financial management. Below you can see what is involved in planning and managing the finances of a business.

Costs, costings and financial performance

Mark and his friend Megan have a sandwich-making business called Double M's *They rent a unit on a small business park and sell directly to shops, petrol stations and local firms, offering working lunches.*

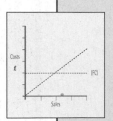

When they first formed the business, they thought about all their start-up costs (e.g. buildings and equipment), and their ongoing running costs. They decided how much money they needed to set up, and drew up a plan to take to the bank in case they needed a loan. Find out more about financial planning on pages 33-35.

Mark and Megan make regular detailed costings, working out their different types of costs, and measuring them against revenue. These calculations show them at what point they break even (all their costs are covered), and help them decide the best price for their products, to give them a reasonable profit. There is more about covering costs on pages 36-38.

They produce monthly cash flow forecasts. The business might be making a profit, but they need to know if there will be enough cash to pay the monthly bills. They draw up business accounts, to show how the figures work (see pages 39-41). You can read about financial statements on pages 42-43.

With all the details in front of them, Mark and Megan can measure the performance of their business. Is it making a reasonable profit, or should they make adjustments to improve the situation? On pages 45-47, you can see how a business carries out checks and comparisons with the figures, to measure its financial performance.

FactZONE

Financial planning - sources of finance

The finance for a business can come from a variety of different sources. Some are better for some kinds of costs, such as start-up costs; others are better for other costs, such as running costs. These different needs (costs) of a business are shown over the page.

Financial sources can be grouped in different ways, e.g. by time period (short-term or long-term). Below is a table which groups them according to whether the finance comes from inside (**internal finance**) or outside the business (**external finance**).

Source	Features	Used for
Internal		
Retained profit	Money saved out of net profit. No interest to pay, easily available. Most common source of finance.	Running costs first. Also, potentially, renewal, expansion.
Investment	Money put in by owners (**owners' capital**) or, if a limited company, obtained by selling shares (**share capital**). Usually long-term commitment.	Start-up costs, buying equipment, renewal, expansion.
Selling / leasing assets	A 'one-off' for raising money, generally when a business is struggling.	Buying equipment, running costs (emergency).
External		
Bank overdrafts	Money allowed to be withdrawn, despite business bank account having negative balance. Short-term agreements, high interest charged.	Covering gaps in cash flow.
Loans	Money from banks or other sources. Arranged to cover different time periods, with different interest rates. Often need guarantees to ensure pay-back.	Start-up costs, buying equipment.
Grants	Money from government, generally tied in to fixed commitments such as improving a region's unemployment or environment.	Start-up costs, buying equipment, expansion.
Trade credit	Buying goods, but not paying for them until an agreed later date. Money is effectively gained in the short term.	Buying stock.
Hire purchase or leasing	Payments are spread over time, so less money committed in the short term. With hire purchase, interest is charged, but item (e.g. equipment) eventually owned outright. With leasing, the item, though never owned, can be updated easily and is often repaired at no cost.	Buying equipment, renewal.

⊚ Financial planning

The careful planning and management of business finance is important at all times, and particularly crucial when a new business is formed. The costs of setting up need to be covered and managers need a clear picture of how they will meet future costs.

You need to know:

■ what finance is needed by businesses in the short and long term

■ the different sources of finance, and those best-suited to meet particular financial needs (see FactZONE, page 33)

■ what goes into a business plan

■ why a business plan is important for people inside and outside a business

Business financial needs can be grouped under four headings:

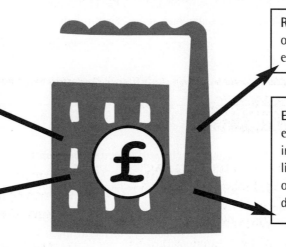

Start-up costs such as the costs of buying a first stock of materials, equipment, e.g. cars, computers, specialist machines, and also, maybe, purchase of premises.

Running costs - the regular costs of producing goods or services, e.g. wages, insurance, electricity, raw materials, rent of premises and, possibly, machinery and petrol for vehicles.

Renewal costs – the costs of repairing and replacing equipment and premises.

Expansion costs – for example, the costs of installing more production lines, employing new staff, opening new premises or developing a new product.

The money needed to cover start-up costs is called **start-up capital**.
The money needed to keep a business going is known as **working capital**
(see also pages 39 and 43).

◎ *Mark and Megan have listed (below) the financial requirements of their sandwich-making business. Sort them into three groups, based on start-up costs, running costs and renewal costs.*

bread-slicing machine	computer for stock checking and accounts
cleaning equipment	bread
expert training for staff	replacement equipment
repairs to van	sandwich fillings
electricity	delivery van
rent on building	workers' wages

Business plans

A **business plan** plays a vital role in financial planning, especially if other organisations, such as banks, are to be asked for loans. It is a formal, detailed document, which explains how the finance for a business is going to be raised. It contains a **cash flow forecast** and projected **financial statements** (see pages 40-44), to show the viability of the business to the banks which are being asked to lend money. A good business plan also includes background information (product or service offered, number of staff, market to be aimed at, etc.) and the targets being set (the business objectives).

Why produce a business plan?

- to avoid costly mistakes
- to set targets for review
- to provide guidelines for managers
- to provide vital information for lenders

The following questions will test your knowledge of financial planning. Make sure you have read this topic through from page 34.

! REMEMBER

Finance involves risks for business owners and for lenders. Will the possible profit outweigh the risk?

Practice questions

1. A group of 18 year-olds ask you, a bank manager, for a £5,000 loan to help start a mobile disco business. They hope to be in profit after a year. What information would you expect to see in their business plan? If you loaned the money, what rules would you make for repayment?

2. For each of these situations, explain which source of finance would be most useful.

    a) A business that wishes to finance a major land purchase for a new factory.
    b) A small taxi firm which needs to buy a new vehicle.
    c) A business which wants to take over a small annexe to add to its rented area, and use it to store more stock.

(?) *For how long would you lend the money? How would you get your money back if the business failed?*

Marks in an exam would be given for your knowledge of different sources of finance, but also for recognizing their suitability for different businesses. Can small businesses afford to pay large amounts of interest? Also, retained profit should always be able to cover running costs, or a business has little chance of survival.

Covering costs

Pages 33-35 looked at the money coming into a business, and what that business must spend money on, including starting up. These two pages now look in more detail at the different kinds of costs incurred by established businesses, and how they work out whether the money coming in from sales alone (**sales revenue**) is enough to cover the money going out. This gives them their 'bottom line' for survival - the break-even point.

You need to know:

■ the meaning of fixed and variable costs

■ how to calculate the break-even point using the contribution method

■ how to identify the break-even point by drawing graphs of costs and revenue

■ the importance of breaking even for business planning

Most businesses look at their general running costs in terms of **fixed costs** and **variable costs**.

REMEMBER

There may not be a 'right' answer to questions about finance. Each business has different factors to consider.

Fixed costs, also called **overheads**. Costs which do not change whatever the number of goods or services produced, e.g. rent on buildings, rates to local councils, interest on loans. These costs will remain the same whatever the level of business activity. (They will only change to any large extent if the business shrinks or expands drastically.)

Variable costs. Costs which change with the amount of goods or services produced, e.g. cost of raw materials, parts, packaging. These costs vary according to the level of business activity.

In the case of some particular costs, such as electricity, transport and wages, what is a fixed cost for one business may be a variable cost for another. Power for a high street bank, for example, can be seen as a fixed cost, whereas power for a launderette is a variable cost, dependent on the amount of times the washing machines are used.

Calculating the break-even point

The managers of a business measure their fixed and variable costs against sales revenue to calculate whether the business will make a loss, make a profit, or break even at different levels of sales. This is crucial information, and is used when making decisions about pricing, cost-cutting, etc. Below are two different methods commonly used by businesses to work out the **break-even point**.

1. The contribution method

This involves a two-part calculation:

a) Price per unit minus cost per unit (variable cost)
    = contribution (to cover fixed costs)

b) Break-even point (level of sales)
    = fixed costs divided by contribution

> **! REMEMBER**
> When you draw graphs, always be careful to add a title, label the axes clearly, and add scales and units.

2. The graph method

1 Plot fixed costs (horizontal line at level of fixed costs). Then plot variable costs (diagonal line showing costs incurred per item produced).

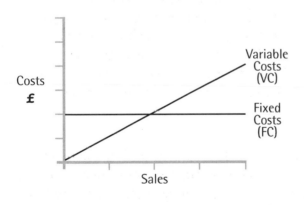

2 Plot total costs line (diagonal line showing total cost incurred per item – fixed and variable combined).

3 Add total revenue line (diagonal line showing revenue obtained per item sold – for this line, the vertical axis represents revenue).

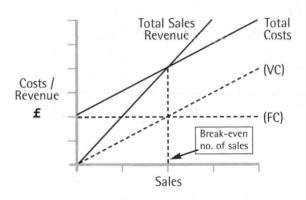

Total costs = fixed costs + (variable cost per unit x number of sales)

Total revenue = price per unit x number of sales

Break-even point is when total costs = total revenue

(?) The manager of a flower shop finds that the business is not breaking even after six months' trading. What could be done to see the business through the next year?

Practice question

The previous two pages have summarised the information you need to revise on covering costs, and calculating break-even. This page gives you a practice question of many parts, based on the *Double M's* case study. Use one or both of the methods of calculating break-even.

Mark and Megan have monthly fixed costs of £1000 for their sandwich business, *Double M's*. The complete cost of producing one sandwich box (their basic product – two rounds of sandwiches and a salad) is £1, and they sell each one for £2.

1. Give an example of *Double M's* fixed costs, and of a variable cost.

2. What does the term break-even mean?

3. How many sandwich boxes need to be sold for *Double M's* to break even?

4. Why is it important that Mark and Megan know this figure?

5. What happens to the break-even point if:

   a) Mark and Megan reduce the price of a box to £1.50?

   b) They discover a cheaper supplier of bread, and the cost of producing a box is reduced to 60p?

   c) Their fixed costs increase to £1200 per month?

(?) For full marks you would need to refer to total costs and total (sales) revenue. Marks would be given for using an appropriate method (contribution or graph method) of calculation, and giving formulae and graph annotations in full. In part 4, you could stress the importance to small firms of knowing when they become profitable, and show the areas which represent profit and loss on a sketched graph (see graph 4 opposite). Remember, lower revenue or higher costs mean more boxes must be sold to break even.
Always show your working out of any calculation on your paper. You can get marks for the right approach even if your answer is wrong.

⦿ Cash flow

Every year thousands of businesses fail as a result of cash flow problems. A firm needs to make sure that it has enough money in the bank to cover its immediate needs.

You need to know:

■ why cash is important to a business

■ the difference between profit and cash

■ why and how businesses draw up cash flow forecasts

Cash flows can be compared to water flowing into and out of a bath. The important task is to keep a reasonable level of water in the bath.

❶ REMEMBER A firm with a profitable future may not survive a cash shortage today.

Cash in

Start-up capital

Cash from sales of goods and services

Bank loans

Grants etc.

Cash out

Raw materials or stock

Fixed costs

Tax payments

Equipment

Wages and salaries etc.

You should never confuse profit and cash in your exam answers. **Profit** is a surplus from trading activities. **Cash** in the bank is a liquid asset that allows a firm to buy the goods and services it needs, add value to them, trade and make profits.

A firm might be making profits, but if it does not have enough cash to pay its **creditors** (people it owes), it can be declared **insolvent** by the courts and may have to cease trading.

Cash flow forecasts

A **cash flow forecast** is a way of trying to predict what money will come in and what money will go out over a fixed period (normally a month). It enables an established business to check whether or not a cash crisis is looming. It is also vital to the business plan presented by a new company to a potential lender. A typical cash flow forecast is generally either a chart (as shown below) or a graph.

On a chart, **cash inflows** (receipts) are listed first, followed by **cash outflows** (payments).

Here is a cash flow forecast chart (of a company with an opening January balance of £0):

	January	February	March	April
CASH IN	9,500	7,000	4,000	4,000
minus				
CASH OUT	7,400	6,500	6,600	5,500
=				
NET CASH FLOW	2,100	500	-2,600	-1,500
plus				
OPENING BALANCE	0	2,100	2,600	0
=				
CLOSING BALANCE	2,100	2,600	0	-1,500

A negative closing balance (a **deficit**) at the end of a month indicates that there is not enough cash to pay the immediate bills.

A regular large **surplus** in the closing balance suggests a business could afford to pay off some debts, or buy new stocks or equipment.

Many firms do not receive payment for their goods or services until one or two months after the sale. These are known as **credit sales**, and clearly affect cash inflow over monthly time periods, just as buying goods on credit (see **trade credit**, page 33) affects cash outflow.

⁇ *A cash flow forecast is an important part of the business plan of a new business. Can you think why a potential lender would want to see it? Why might it be advisable for a new business to arrange an overdraft quickly?*

(?) *A medium-sized business has lost £30 000 during the last 6 months. If you were asked to advise them, what would their cash flow forecasts tell you, and what conclusions could you draw?*

Remember, past cash flow forecasts will give you an idea of actual demand for goods or services.

! REMEMBER
Always explain yourself. If you suggest something that might improve cash flow, say **why** you think it might.

Practice question

A soft toy company, *Fuzz*, has drawn up an actual cash flow graph for the last sixmonths' trading, to compare with its cash flow forecast for the same period.

1. What does the cash flow forecast graph show?

2. How did the actual cash flow differ from the forecast?

3. What problems might these differences cause for *Fuzz*?

4. How might *Fuzz* improve its cash flow?

(?) *Examiners want to see if you can interpret cash flow graphs (or charts). Show that you understand that negative items represent a deficit (where outflow was greater than inflow). Identify and try to explain trends - when does cash flow appear to improve? Why might this be the case for a soft toy company? For parts 3 and 4, will the company have enough cash for its coming needs – and if not, how might this be remedied?*

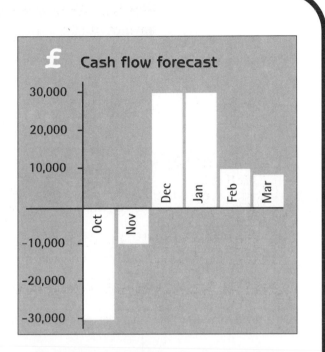

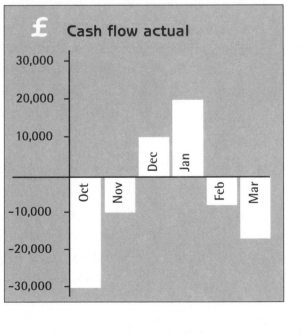

ⓉⓋ Financial statements

All businesses, whatever their size, need to have an efficient system for keeping track of their money. The financial statements kept by the business, and which make up its **accounts**, are records of all the financial transactions with which it is involved.

You need to know:

■ what is recorded in a profit and loss account

■ why a balance sheet has to balance.

■ why firms have to record financial transactions

The **profit and loss account** and the **balance sheet** are the two main financial statements (there are examples on these two pages). Both provide information on what a business has been doing in the recent past, and how these activities have been paid for. This information, which can be compared with figures from previous years, helps those involved in the business make decisions about the future.

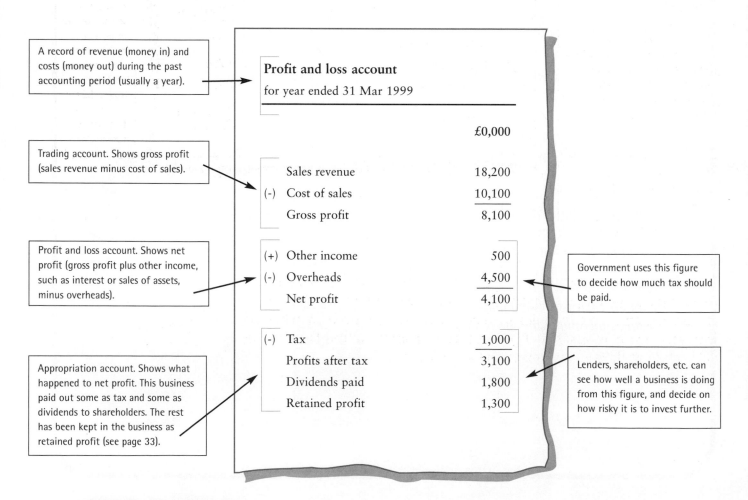

A record of revenue (money in) and costs (money out) during the past accounting period (usually a year).

Trading account. Shows gross profit (sales revenue minus cost of sales).

Profit and loss account. Shows net profit (gross profit plus other income, such as interest or sales of assets, minus overheads).

Appropriation account. Shows what happened to net profit. This business paid out some as tax and some as dividends to shareholders. The rest has been kept in the business as retained profit (see page 33).

Profit and loss account

for year ended 31 Mar 1999

		£0,000
	Sales revenue	18,200
(-)	Cost of sales	10,100
	Gross profit	8,100
(+)	Other income	500
(-)	Overheads	4,500
	Net profit	4,100
(-)	Tax	1,000
	Profits after tax	3,100
	Dividends paid	1,800
	Retained profit	1,300

Government uses this figure to decide how much tax should be paid.

Lenders, shareholders, etc. can see how well a business is doing from this figure, and decide on how risky it is to invest further.

A record of the value of what a firm owns (its **assets**), the value of what it owes (its **liabilities**) and the value of the capital invested in the firm. It is a 'snapshot' taken at a particular point in time (usually the last day of the accounting period).

Assets such as buildings and equipment. There may be different views of how much such things are worth.

Assets which are easily turned into cash.

Debts to be repaid within one year, e.g. short-term loans.

Current assets minus current liabilities.

Total assets minus current liabilities.

Long-term loans, etc. Balance sheet layout varies between firms – for instance, these liabilities, instead of being subtracted here, are often added to the capital and reserves section below.

Owners' or share capital, retained profit, loans, grants, etc. – see page 33.

The figures must balance. The accountant must ensure that the 'where is the money now' and the 'where did the money come from' boxes actually tally.

Balance sheet

as at 31 Mar 1999

	£0,000	£0,000
Assets		
Fixed assets		3,400
Current assets		
Stock	800	
Debtors	2,100	
Cash	2,300	
	5,200	
Liabilities		
Current liabilities	3,800	
Net current assets (working capital)		1,400
Net assets employed		4800
Long-term liabilities	1,800	
		3,000
Capital & reserves		
Share capital		1,700
Retained profit		1,300
Capital employed		3,000

Small firms draw up their own financial statements or pay an accountant to do it for them. Larger companies have their own finance department and accountants. All companies are required by law to provide shareholders with accounting information. Public limited companies do this through the publication of their annual report and accounts.

44

The questions below test your knowledge of financial statements. Make sure you have read pages 42 and 43 thoroughly, but try not to refer to them as you compose your answers.

(?) *You are an accountant friend of Mark and Megan, owners of Double Ms. They have asked you about financial statements. Can you think how to answer their questions?*

What will tell us whether or not we can expand?

What will tell us whether or not we can pay off our debts?

Practice question

On the right you can see a balance sheet of the company *Property Ltd.*

1. Fill in the missing figures for working capital and loans.
   Show your working out.

2. Give one example of a fixed asset and of a current liability

3. Explain the purpose of a balance sheet.

4. Explain the purpose of a profit and loss account.

(?) *For part 1, write a complete answer, with words as well as figures. For a current liability in part 2, think about the different ways the business might have borrowed money. For parts 3 and 4, think of who might use the information presented.*

PROPERTY LTD

Balance sheet as at 31.3.99

	£0,000	£0,000
Fixed assets		140
Current assets		
Stock	40	
Debtors	10	
Cash	50	
	100	
Current liabilities	75	
Working capital	?	
Net assets employed		165
Share capital	50	
Retained profit	60	
Loans (long-term)	?	
Capital employed		165

Financial performance

Businesses need to be constantly aware of the condition of their finances, so that they can try to make adjustments where necessary to keep afloat. One way managers can keep an eye on things is to carry out performance checks - taking the accounts information for the past year and doing some comparisons and investigations with the figures.

You need to know:

■ why businesses want to use performance measures such as ratios

■ how to work out the three profitability ratios and two liquidity ratios

■ how to interpret these ratios

■ the different groups of people who might use such ratios

Managers need to have more precise knowledge about a company's profitability and liquidity than just whether it is making money and whether it has enough cash to pay off its debts. More helpful information - for instance, whether it is making enough money given the level of sales or money invested, or what percentage of available cash would be needed to pay off its debts - is provided by **performance ratios**. These are described on pages 46 and 47.

An example of the information gained from a performance ratio is shown here:

■ In their fourth year of trading, *Double M*'s sandwiches have sales of £45 000 with a gross profit of £27 000 (figures taken from their profit and loss account).

■ Calculating their gross profit margin (as shown on page 47) shows Mark and Megan that they are making £3 in gross profit for every £5 of sales (they have a 3:5, or 60%, gross profit margin).

■ They can compare these figures with those from previous years, and those of other businesses.

Performance ratios

To check financial performance, certain ratios need to be calculated. They are worked out by comparing different pairs of figures in the accounts (see pages 42-43) that are related in some way. Each ratio gives slightly different information about the **profitability** or **liquidity** of a business. Look at the ratios in the FactZONE opposite, and then try the questions below.

(see pages 42-43)

(?) *Why might a small business regularly check its stock and measure its gross profit margins?*

Remember, stock sitting in a back room for long is not 'paying its way'. What is a gross profit margin useful for?

!   REMEMBER

Ratios are based on past figures - they can help with forecasts but will not guarantee results.

46

Practice question

Examine this extract from a balance sheet of *West Stores plc.*

1. Calculate the company's current ratio.

2. What does this ratio tell you about the success of the company?

(?) *In a ratio question, you will get some marks for linking the right figures, and full marks for showing the ratio in its simplest form, e.g. (3:1). For a question like part 2, if a ratio is very high or very low, comment on problems and what might be done about them.*

Balance sheet as at 31.3.98		
	£0,000	£0,000
Fixed assets		13,000
Current assets		
Stock	3,880	
Debtors	40	
Cash	80	
	4,000	
Current liabilities		
Creditors	720	
Overdraft	80	
	800	

FactZONE

Ratio	What does it show?	Who might be interested?
Profitability		
Gross profit margin Gross profit : sales revenue $\dfrac{\text{Gross profit}}{\text{Sales revenue}}$ x 100 %	How much gross profit for every £1 of sales. The bigger the %, the greater the profit.	Managers - is the firm performing well? Creditors - are profits enough to allow loans to be repaid?
Net profit margin Net profit : sales revenue $\dfrac{\text{Net profit}}{\text{Sales revenue}}$ x 100 %	As before, but now allowing for fixed costs.	As before.
Return on capital employed (ROCE) Net profit : capital employed $\dfrac{\text{Net profit}}{\text{Capital employed}}$ x 100 %	What profit is created from each £1 invested.	Shareholders (investors) - is investment providing as good a return as other options might?
Liquidity		
Current ratio Current assets : current liabilities	Shows how easily a firm's short-term debts could be paid from current assets. Ratio of 1:1 means a firm is only just covering debts. Ratio of 3:1 means firm has 3x the money needed to cover debts. This is wasteful of money which could be used to buy machinery, etc.	Managers, creditors - how easily can the firm's debts be covered? Linked to cash flow forecasts (see page 40).
Acid test ratio Current assets - stock : current liabilities	Current assets figures include stocks, which might be hard to turn into ready cash. Acid test, which removes them from the equation, is a more realistic measure. A reasonable figure is seen as between 0.5:1 and 1:1.	As before.

People in business

This section is about:

- What motivates people to work

- How new staff are recruited

- Training staff

- Communication in the workplace

- Industrial relations

In a small business, the responsibility for recruiting, training and getting on well together is likely to be held by the manager, and good practice just seems like common sense. In a large business there is an entire Human Resources department, generally responsible for all aspects of people management. Below you can see what a typical day in the life of a Human Resources manager might be like.

A typical day for a Human Resources manager

Kim works as a Human Resources manager at the head office of a computer company which has a number of shops across the Midlands.

Kim has been asked to draw up a report on the results of a new bonus pay scheme. You can find out more about motivation to work on pages 49-51. She also needs to sort through some job applications with the finance manager, and arrange some interviews. For more on recruitment, see pages 52-55.

Today, a group of new sales staff begin work. Kim will be helping to train them. This morning she will give each one a contract of employment, show them around and introduce them to their new colleagues. More about training staff can be found on pages 56-57.

There have been complaints about the new teams into which people have been placed in the despatch department. Kim will have to set up a meeting with all those affected before deciding whether to make any changes. Communication at work is described on pages 58-60.

Some staff give computer help and advice over the telephone all day. Kim has a meeting today with management and Trade Union representatives to discuss teleworking from home for these employees. You can find out more about industrial relations on pages 61-65.

During the day Kim will also need to deal with a number of telephone calls, carry out a health and safety check on the office areas and spend a bit of time on arrangements for the staff Christmas party.

FactZONE

Motivation – Maslow's Hierarchy of Needs

Abraham Maslow (1908-1970) did some research on why people work. He drew up his 'Hierarchy of Needs' pyramid from his findings. He ranked people's needs in order of importance, the most basic needs being at the bottom of the pyramid, and the more advanced needs being at the top.

The pyramid represents the things that motivate us to work. Starting at the bottom, the first thing is a basic need to have food and shelter. Once this is being satisfied, it no longer motivates us by itself, and so we move up a level. On the next level most of us have safety needs, which means we look for things like job security. Once these needs are satisfied, we move up another level, and so on.

☐ **Maslow's needs can be learnt as the '5 Ss'**

! REMEMBER
Theories like Maslow's give you a different way of looking at behaviour. Not everyone will fit exactly into his hierarchy in the same way.

Increasing importance

- **S**elf-fulfilment needs (reaching your potential)
- Self-esteem needs (a sense of **S**tatus)
- **S**ocial needs (relationships with other workers)
- **S**afety needs, e.g. job security, pension
- Basic needs / **S**urvival, e.g. food and shelter or the money to obtain these

Other important names

Elton Mayo (1880-1949) believed an employee's attitude was more important than anything else. Increasing a worker's personal satisfaction was the best form of motivation.

Douglas McGregor studied managers' views of their employees. Two distinct views emerged:

1) Theory X - that workers don't like working, are just after money, and that everyone needs to be closely supervised.

2) Theory Y - that workers enjoy work, can be trusted and are motivated by things such as job satisfaction.

In MacGregor's view, a firm would work more successfully if the managers subscribed to theory Y.

Motivation

Motivation at work means providing encouragement and **incentives** (things which make people want to work). Much research has been put into investigating why people work, and the best motivating factors. The FactZONE on page 49 shows the main theories on the subject.

You need to know:

■ the theories used to explain why people work

■ the ways in which businesses try to encourage individual and team work

■ the methods used to pay workers

■ why different types of payment suit different jobs

◎ *Below are some of the things that may affect people's commitment to the work they do. Businesses use such things to encourage better work. Try putting them in order of importance to you personally (picture yourself in your first full-time job). How does your list compare with Maslow's Hierarchy of Needs, shown in the FactZONE on page 49?*

Financial incentives

■ being paid a good wage
■ bonus payments, e.g. for meeting targets
■ fringe benefits, e.g. free meals
■ extra payments, such as overtime
■ commission, e.g. for the number of goods sold
■ a contract for 5 years

Non-financial incentives

■ varied and interesting work
■ being given responsibility to make decisions
■ being praised for good work
■ having the opportunity for promotion
■ feeling valued because comments are listened to
■ working with other people in a good environment
■ feeling challenged by the work

Practice question

What factors should a business consider when deciding how to design jobs and how to reward its staff?

(?) *Think about Maslow's hierarchy and the financial and non-financial incentives. How can they be built into a job? Don't forget to say **why** the different factors should be considered, e.g. people should be put in teams **because** workers have been shown to work better in a good social environment.*

Motivation and pay

There are several different ways in which workers can be paid. Different systems of pay may encourage or discourage the efforts of different workers, so a business needs to be careful to be fair to everyone.

Different types of payment

- **Wages** and **salaries** - wages (most manual workers) are based on hourly rates, and are normally paid weekly. Salaries (most non-manual workers) are based on yearly figures, and paid directly into bank accounts each month. In both cases, Income tax (PAYE in Britain) and National Insurance are deducted by the employer, and paid to the government. Some governments have set a national minimum (basic) wage.
- **Time rate** - payment for the time taken to complete the job. May encourage workers to take longer to finish, as tasks could be lengthened.
- **Overtime** - payment when a job cannot be completed in the normal time, often paid at a higher rate than normal.
- **Piece rate** - payment by the number of products finished. Can encourage speed but may lead to poor quality.
- **Bonus payments** - extra payments if a job is finished early or by a deadline.
- **Commission** - payment of a (low) basic wage plus a percentage of the value of items sold or made. Common practice in sales departments.
- **Performance-related pay** - another type of 'payment by results', where pay is linked to achievement of targets. Difficult to use in jobs where 'achievement of targets' is not easily measured (e.g. nurses caring for different numbers of patients, with different levels of need).
- **Profit-sharing** - extra payments based on company profit over a given period.

As well as these different types of payment, **fringe benefits** (extra goods/services) may be offered, e.g. company cars, pensions, private healthcare, and cheap loans. Managers are likely to receive more of these than workers.

> **!** R E M E M B E R
> The best payment system for a firm may not be the best system for a worker.

◎ *Decide which pay system (or systems) might suit each of the following workers and jot down your reasons why: a cleaner, a mobile phone salesman, a nurse, a Post Office counter clerk and a lorry driver.*

Practice question

Some employees have suggested to their boss that less money should be spent on staff training and on bonuses, and that the saving from this should be used to increase hourly pay rates. Analyse the effect this might have on staff motivation.

(?) *Do you think all staff would benefit to the same degree from a general pay rise? Where might motivation be lost? How might the employer gain or lose?*

ⓉⓋ Recruitment

The process of finding new staff for a company, from advertising jobs to signing contracts, needs to be well run if it is not to waste valuable company time. Choosing the right person for a job depends, to a large degree, on getting the right procedures and documents in place.

You need to know:

■ the main stages involved in a recruitment process

■ what is contained in the different documents involved in recruitment

■ what these documents are used for

❗ REMEMBER Businesses may have their own recruitment processes but their job adverts have to be fair and open to everyone with the right skills.

The typical stages in the recruitment process of a medium to large company are outlined below (they may differ slightly from business to business). A small company may well not follow all the same procedures.

1. The manager of the department with the vacancy consults the Human Resources manager. They draw up two key documents - the **job description** and the **person specification**.
2. The job advertisement is placed in the local paper. After the application deadline has passed, application forms and CVs are checked to remove obviously unsuitable people. The rest of the applications are compared to the person specification to arrive at a shortlist for interview.
3. The candidates are interviewed, and may be given a test of some kind to do. The job is offered to the most suitable (if no candidate proves suitable, the job will be re-advertised). Unsuccessful candidates are notified.
4. The successful candidate's references are checked. If any problems arise, the job may be offered to the next most suitable person from the list. If all their references are fine, a time is set for the new person to start.
5. A contract and some induction training are arranged. The performance of the new staff member will be monitored through an **appraisal system** - manager and worker will agree on targets for a set period and then review the results.

⁇ *Can you think which of these stages the manager of a small hair salon might do away with, or replace? What more informal methods might she use?*

◎ *Flow charts like the one below are useful revision aids. See if you can draw one to summarise the 5 stages shown above (cover the text first). The first step has been done for you here:*

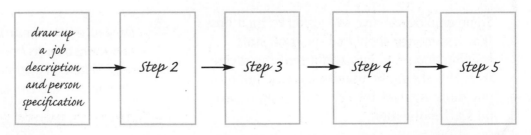

| draw up a job description and person specification | → | Step 2 | → | Step 3 | → | Step 4 | → | Step 5 |

FactZONE

The Human Resources department must plan ahead, identify and fill job vacancies.

Why might a vacancy arise?

- worker(s) may be due for retirement
- worker(s) may leave for other reasons
- worker(s) may be promoted
- business expansion may create new jobs

Job description

A **job description** is drawn up by an employer. It lists all the duties an employee must carry out in that particular job, as well as:

- the job title
- who they are responsible to
- who they are in charge of

Job advertisement

A **job advertisement** is written by an employer. It contains details of a position to be filled, and where to apply. It may be:

- internal – only circulated within the business in order to give existing staff the chance to apply.
- external – published in appropriate places, e.g. local, national or specialist newspapers. Also possibly sent to Job Centres and recruitment agencies.

Person specification

A **person specification** is drawn up by an employer. It gives a picture of the ideal candidate for a job, and is used to help decide on the most suitable person for that job. It contains things like:

- qualifications required
- previous experience needed
- special skills needed, e.g. speaking a foreign language
- type of personality needed, e.g. good telephone manner and confidence with the public for a receptionist job

Curriculum Vitae

A **CV** (**curriculum vitae**) is written by a job applicant. It lists their qualifications, interests and experience, and is normally laid out like this:

- name
- date of birth
- address
- telephone number
- educational qualifications
- previous jobs (listed backwards, that is, starting with the most recent one)
- interests
- names of referees (one of which is usually the last employer, or the headteacher if the applicant is a school leaver)

Practice question

This two-page question gives you an example of an extended case study question, the type of exam question where you are given material that you must read and understand in order to answer the questions at the end:

Study all the information here, and use it to give full answers to the questions that follow.

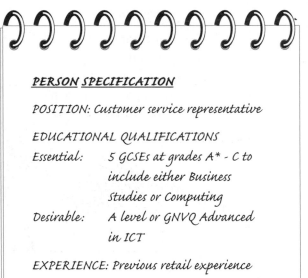

Kim works for a computer company called *Bytes*, which sells from retail outlets and by mail order, and gives full after-sales support. She needs someone to work at the main warehouse, running the shop at the front and also giving advice and technical support to customers over the phone.

Kim first worked with a colleague to draw up the job description and person specification shown below. Having tried to recruit internally without success, she then rang the local paper and placed an advertisement. She has now narrowed down her shortlist to two candidates. Their CVs are shown opposite.

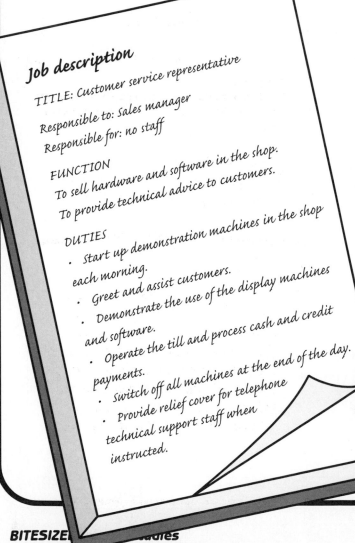

Job description

TITLE: Customer service representative

Responsible to: Sales manager
Responsible for: no staff

FUNCTION
To sell hardware and software in the shop.
To provide technical advice to customers.

DUTIES
- Start up demonstration machines in the shop each morning.
- Greet and assist customers.
- Demonstrate the use of the display machines and software.
- Operate the till and process cash and credit payments.
- Switch off all machines at the end of the day.
- Provide relief cover for telephone technical support staff when instructed.

PERSON SPECIFICATION

POSITION: Customer service representative

EDUCATIONAL QUALIFICATIONS
Essential: 5 GCSEs at grades A* - C to include either Business Studies or Computing
Desirable: A level or GNVQ Advanced in ICT

EXPERIENCE: Previous retail experience preferred

SPECIAL SKILLS: An interest in computers and good knowledge of current market for PCs and software

PERSONALITY: Polite, pleasant personality

Curriculum Vitae

PAULA TAIT
10th June 1982

10, High Street,
Evesham

___

QUALIFICATIONS

GCSE   English B
          French A
          Maths D
          Science C
          Business Studies C

EMPLOYMENT
1998 to date: Sales assistant, Woolworths,
Evesham

INTERESTS
Riding, walking

REFERENCES
Headteacher, Courtmoor School, Evesham

CURRICULUM VITAE

Karen Lewis
29th May 1982

The Pines,
Main Street,
Evesham

Qualifications

GCSE	English	C
	Maths	C
	ICT	A
	Business Studies	B
	Art	C
GNVQ	Intermediate Business	merit

Employment
To date 3 weeks work experience at a computer
shop, plus Saturday work this year at the same
shop.

Interests
Music, computing

References
The manager, Your PC, Evesham

Now answer these questions:

1. If you were Human Resources manager at *Bytes* which of the two candidates would you call to interview and why?

2. List six questions you would ask at interview.

3. What does the term 'recruit internally' mean? What are the advantages of this method?

(?) *Remember, good questions help a candidate to talk, and bring out information that is not on a CV. Think about questions which can test the candidate's skills and attitudes to work, and find out if their experience will be useful. For part 3, think about advantages for staff and employer.*

ⓉⓋ Training staff

Training is a very important business activity. Both new and experienced staff benefit from developing their skills and learning new ones.

You need to know:

■ why training is of benefit to both employers and employees

■ the different kinds of training offered by businesses

■ how government schemes can help

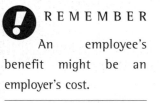

The first week at work

Karen receives her staff handbook on her first day. She is shown around and meets her new colleagues. She watches a video about the company and is shown how to use the display computers and the till. Every Wednesday, Karen goes to a lecture at college, as part of her NVQ course.

◎ *All Karen's training activities (above) are either on-the-job or off-the-job training. Try drawing spider diagrams like the one below to show the costs and benefits of on-the-job or off-the-job training.*

❗ REMEMBER

An employee's benefit might be an employer's cost.

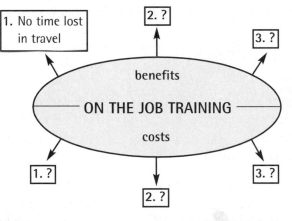

1. No time lost in travel

2. ?

3. ?

benefits

ON THE JOB TRAINING

costs

1. ?

2. ?

3. ?

A spider diagram is a good way of organising your facts for revision. You could draw one up like this.

Practice question

A new finance control software package is available for businesses to buy. Why might a company prefer to pay for off-the-job training to teach its employees to use this system (instead of training them on-the-job)?

❓ *Think about the company's resources – time, money, skills, knowledge. Will this be one-off training or might it need updating later?*

FactZONE

Why train?

- continued training is essential, because the business environment is constantly changing. Workers need to acquire new skills and work flexibility.
- a business with a good training reputation will be respected by staff, other employers and customers.
- properly trained staff:
  - are more productive and satisfied in their work
  - take less time off and stay longer with a business, becoming experienced and highly skilled.
  - are confident of their ability and more likely to obtain promotion.

Types of training

Induction training – training given to new employees. As well as teaching basic job skills, it introduces the employees to the business and its expectations (it might include a company presentation, e.g. a company video).

On-the-job training – training given whilst employees are working. This might involve an employee being **coached**, or guided through a process. It might also involve **mentoring**, which is where an employee does the job but is teamed up with an experienced person (to discuss problems and progress with). Skilled training staff may also organize activities, e.g. visits to other companies, group problem-solving tasks or role playing, where trainees can experience events in the role of customer, manager, etc.

Off-the-job training – specialist training which involves employees stopping their usual work. It may be provided by another company and may be done at a training centre away from the usual place of work.

Government schemes have been set up to improve workers' qualifications and help unemployed people get back to work:

> **Training and Enterprise Councils (TECs)** have been set up to manage training in regional areas. They promote training awards for businesses. The **Investors in People (IIP)** award recognizes quality training in businesses which set high standards, involve staff and evaluate their own success regularly.

> **NVQs (National Vocational Qualifications)** are qualifications awarded to people acquiring sets of skills required for specific jobs. These skills are assessed in the workplace and must meet set standards. Different levels of NVQ range from beginner to university-level work.

> About seven million adults in the UK have no formal qualifications and one in five people has poor literacy and numeracy skills. The government has introduced a 'welfare to work' programme, aimed at younger people and the long-term unemployed, which will stop people claiming welfare benefits unless they join training programmes.

What do you think are the potential benefits to a business of providing staff training?

📺 Communication at work

Good communication is vital in the workplace. Information needs to move in the right direction, in the right form and to the right people if a business is to succeed.

You need to know:

■ the different ways in which information is passed between groups and individuals

■ which methods of communication are suitable for which situations

■ what ICT means to the modern business world.

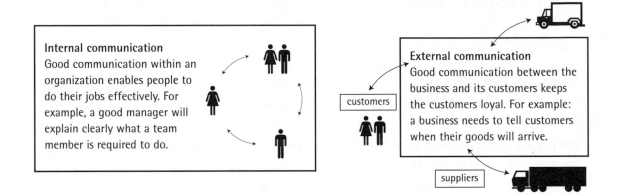

Internal communication
Good communication within an organization enables people to do their jobs effectively. For example, a good manager will explain clearly what a team member is required to do.

External communication
Good communication between the business and its customers keeps the customers loyal. For example: a business needs to tell customers when their goods will arrive.

customers

suppliers

❓ *In the examples below, there have been communication problems. How might these situations have happened? How could they have been prevented?*

Think about which types of communication have been involved. Have internal errors led to external ones? Are people talking to everyone they should do?

Consumer Line your questions answered

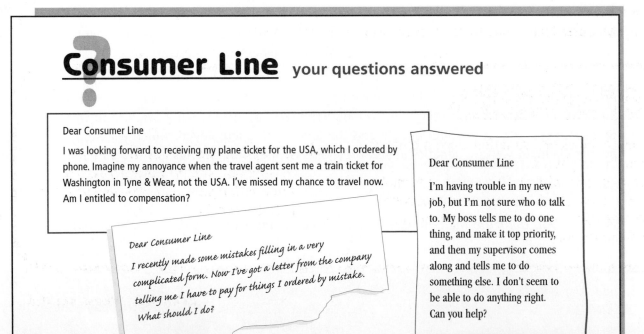

Dear Consumer Line

I was looking forward to receiving my plane ticket for the USA, which I ordered by phone. Imagine my annoyance when the travel agent sent me a train ticket for Washington in Tyne & Wear, not the USA. I've missed my chance to travel now. Am I entitled to compensation?

Dear Consumer Line

I recently made some mistakes filling in a very complicated form. Now I've got a letter from the company telling me I have to pay for things I ordered by mistake. What should I do?

Dear Consumer Line

I'm having trouble in my new job, but I'm not sure who to talk to. My boss tells me to do one thing, and make it top priority, and then my supervisor comes along and tells me to do something else. I don't seem to be able to do anything right. Can you help?

Channels of communication

The way a message is passed is called the **channel of communication**. Some different channels are shown here:

Written channels	**Verbal channels**
memos letters e-mail fax notices reports Written communications provide a permanent record	meetings telephone calls conversations presentations public address systems Verbal communications provide speedy feedback and are especially good for negotiations.

The success of messages and the feedback they provoke depends largely on organisation and whether the right type of message is used for the right direction.

For instance, notices used as 'downwards' messages (from management to staff), reports used as 'upwards' messages (from staff to management), and memos and e-mail notes used as 'sideways' messages (between colleagues) all work because they go in the right direction. But a notice, for example, would not be the correct way for the workforce to communicate with the management.

Information and communications technology (ICT) has caused a great change in the way some people work. Many routine tasks can now be done quickly and easily with a **personal computer**, using word processing, spreadsheets and databases. With a **modem**, information can be sent through the telephone network, giving **e-mail** facilities and access to the **Internet**. Modems are also vital to the growing number of **teleworkers** in the workforce today. These are employees who work away from their place of employment (normally at home), and use computer technology to connect them to their employers.

REMEMBER
In a competitive business world, speed is extremely important in most communication.

Practice question

Give examples of a situation when a business manager might use the following to communicate with staff: a memo, a formal report, a circular letter, a personal meeting. When might these be the wrong types of communication to use?

Think about who needs to know the information and how urgently. Is the information personal? How important is it to the receiver?

Writing a report

Depending on your syllabus, you may need to know how to set out, for example, a letter replying to a customer complaint, an internal memo or a formal report to a meeting.

◎ *Read the ICT text on page 59. Look at the following report layout and take note of its structure. Then cover it up, and write your own brief report, explaining how advances in ICT have changed the way companies communicate information.*

❗ REMEMBER

ICT can speed up communications, but customers still need carefully thought-out messages with personal touches.

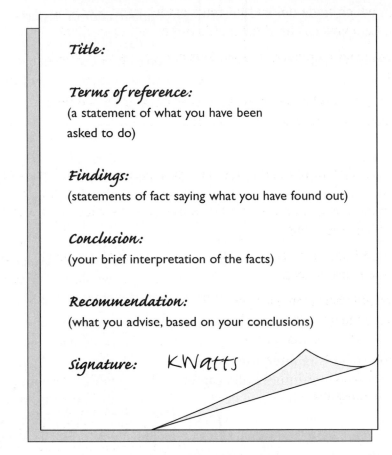

Title:

Terms of reference:
(a statement of what you have been asked to do)

Findings:
(statements of fact saying what you have found out)

Conclusion:
(your brief interpretation of the facts)

Recommendation:
(what you advise, based on your conclusions)

Signature: KWatts

Practice question

What are the main advantages and disadvantages of teleworking for:

  a) the employer?
  b) the employee?

(?) *It would be a good idea to use an example here, so you can illustrate your general points by applying them to one business. Think what an employer gains when workers do not have to come together to one place between 9.00am and 5.00pm. Think about the effects on communication and motivation.*

Industrial relations

Industrial relations is the term used to describe the relationship between the workforce and the management of a business. In any business, issues involving staff and management might be small day-to-day ones like lateness or sorting out job roles, but there are also important issues like pay negotiations or the introduction of new working methods, which affect the whole of a workforce.

You need to know:

■ the ways in which trade unions and trade associations represent workers and employers, and the benefits of belonging to them

■ the different ways employers and workers can successfully reach agreements

■ the kinds of action taken by employers, workers and their unions, and by outside groups, to sort out conflicts

REMEMBER
Industrial relations isn't just about strikes. It is about employers and workers working together to solve a range of problems.

All businesses need to have good industrial relations. An extreme measure, such as a strike, can be disastrous – there are costs for both the business, in lost production and customers, and the workers, as they lose wages and, in some situations, their jobs.

The diagram and questions below will help you to think about how groups might settle their differences.

These workers and their employer are from a company making pre-packed cakes to sell to supermarkets. To stay in business, the cakes need to be made faster and at less cost. Talks on pay and machines are being held.

Think what everyone might agree about. How might each group have to change its demands to reach agreement?

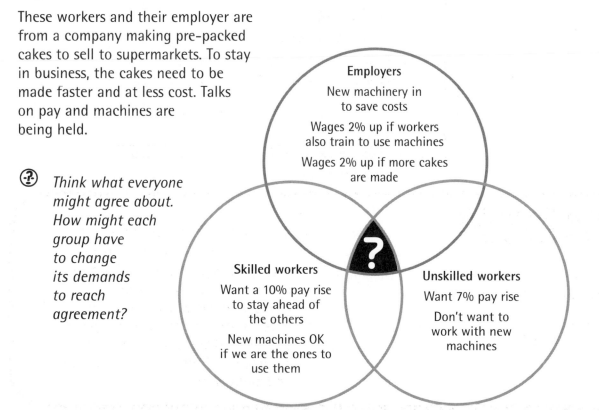

Employers
New machinery in to save costs

Wages 2% up if workers also train to use machines

Wages 2% up if more cakes are made

Skilled workers
Want a 10% pay rise to stay ahead of the others

New machines OK if we are the ones to use them

Unskilled workers
Want 7% pay rise

Don't want to work with new machines

BITESIZEbusiness studies

Negotiating

Most industries and businesses decide pay and other issues by **collective bargaining** (negotiating as a group rather than as an individual). The trade unions and trade associations negotiate, and make decisions for all their members.

Trade unions are organizations that look after the interests of the workers. Many people join a union because the union will negotiate on their behalf, dealing with issues such as pay, hours of work, holiday entitlement, redundancy and job security.

Trade associations speak on behalf of employers. They can negotiate pay, present the industry's view to the public, and provide advice for firms large and small. There are over 100 large associations and many more smaller ones. Employers as a whole are represented by the CBI (Confederation of British Industry).

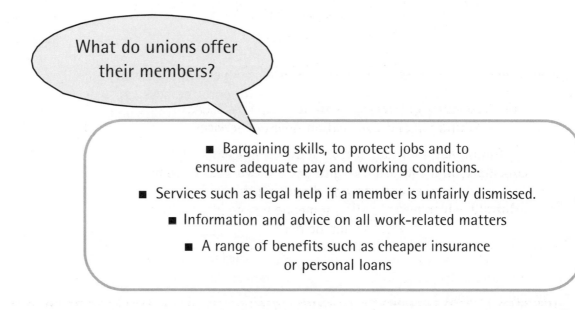

What do unions offer their members?

- Bargaining skills, to protect jobs and to ensure adequate pay and working conditions.

- Services such as legal help if a member is unfairly dismissed.

- Information and advice on all work-related matters

- A range of benefits such as cheaper insurance or personal loans

Bargaining may be done at a national level, as with a nationwide industry, or at a local level, with, for example, a small firm's union representative (sometimes called the **shop steward**) bargaining with management on behalf of company workers. Generally, different unions within a company will have their own representatives, who negotiate for their own workers.

However, some Far Eastern companies with factories in the UK have introduced new-style agreements with just a **single union** to represent all workers.

Some firms ask workers to sign **no-strike agreements** and put more emphasis on teamwork.

Industrial action

If negotiations fail then the union can call for its members to take industrial action, to try to put pressure on the management to accept the union's point of view. Unions must ask for their members' opinions through a **secret ballot** (vote) before taking industrial action. Such action might involve a:

■ strike (all workers stop work)

■ ban on doing overtime

■ boycott (refusing to do particular tasks)

■ work to rule (doing only those specific tasks which are outlined in your contract)

> What happens when agreement can't be reached?

The business might decide to ask for help from ACAS (the Arbitration and Conciliation Advisory Service).

This organization can provide independent people to:
conciliate, which means trying to get the two sides to come together and carry on discussing things,
arbitrate, which means letting someone independent decide what should be done.

! REMEMBER

An outside agency might recommend a compromise, but it might also conclude that one side's argument should be supported (and not the other's).

Practice questions

1. How might a large firm making chocolate bars be affected by these kinds of industrial action:

   a) an overtime ban
   b) a work to rule by some workers
   c) an all-out strike

2. Why might a Single Union agreement be good for both employers and workers in a large firm?

❓ *Think about how a large production line works. What will happen if one section of workers is missing or working very slowly? Can an employer keep production going in some way? What if he can't?*

Think what it would be like for workers and employers discussing a pay rise with five different unions involved.

Practice question

Study all the information below, and use it to give full answers to the questions that follow.

Remember, with a case study question always read all the material carefully, as you will be marked on your ability to interpret the information and use it to make judgements and come to conclusions.

The team of teleworkers at the computer company *Bytes* work on the telephone, giving advice to customers with computer problems. The management would like some of them to work from home rather than from the office. They believe this would be a good chance to extend the hours that the support line is available to customers, by asking some of the staff to change the hours they work as well as their place of work.

As Kim, the Human Resources manager, prepares the contract of employment, she needs to consult the union representative to make sure that the terms being offered are fair to the staff. The staff involved belong to a union called the Union of Shop Distributive and Allied Workers (USDAW).

Kim and the union representative put forward the views of the management and the affected staff respectively. They will try to get the best possible working arrangements in place, and are both aware that compromises will probably have to be made. Here are some of the things they say in discussion:

Kim

Staff choosing to work from home must change their hours. There will be two new shifts: 7.00am - 3.00pm and 2.00pm - 10.00pm.

There will be no increase in pay for shift work.

Staff must come in to the office at least once a week to attend a team briefing.

Some phone calls will be monitored to check the quality of advice given and the number of calls taken.

Only those who volunteer for teleworking at home should have to do it.

Staff should not be asked to work different shifts.

Extra pay should be given for overtime.

Bytes should provide all equipment for working at home.

Contracts of employment should be permanent no matter where you work.

USDAW representitive

Now answer these questions:

1. Why does Kim want teleworkers to change their working hours?
2. What might the union representative expect in return for changing working hours?
3. What action might each side take if they fail to agree?
4. What advice might an outside service like ACAS offer to the company?

(?) *Think about what the employer gains and loses. Unions might give way on one issue but if so, will push hard on other issues. If no-one will give way, what might both sides threaten?*

FactZONE

Industrial relations, employment and the law

There have been many changes in the workplace in recent years. Few employers can offer a guaranteed job for life and many firms would prefer to take workers as and when they need them. All employers in this country must still comply with the Employment Laws, though.

Things an employer must do

- Provide a written statement on pay, holidays and period of employment
- Give equal pay to men and women if they are doing the same work
- Give specific benefits to workers who have completed two years with the firm
- Follow health and safety laws (Health and Safety at Work Act, 1974).

Things an employer must not do

- Discriminate against workers because of their race, age, gender (sex) or disability (Equal Opportunities Laws)
- Stop a worker from belonging to a trade union
- Employ children under 13
- Dismiss a worker unfairly

Health and safety points to remember

For the exam, you are not expected to know the particular name and dates of each law affecting the workplace. But you do need to be able to explain what is expected of firms in terms of health and safety and equal opportunities:

- Employers must provide fire escapes, safety guards on machines and good toilets. Good overall hygiene standards should be kept.
- Employers and employees should take reasonable care to look after their own and others' safety.
- Employers must identify harmful tasks and minimize risks.

Equal opportunities points to remember

Employers must show no discrimination on grounds of race, age, gender or disability in their:

- selection procedures
- contracts
- training
- benefits
- redundancies

❗ REMEMBER

A lot of firms protect their workers with policies which are better than the law asks for. These policies cost money but workers give extra loyalty to good employers.

Business and marketing

This section is about:

- Market research

- The marketing mix

- Product life cycles

- Pricing decisions

- Promoting products

In a very competitive business world, it is usually not enough to design and make a good product. The product needs to be marketed, so that consumers find out about it and are attracted to buy it. Companies spend a significant proportion of their budget on marketing their products, so getting it right is important.

The market and marketing

Most firms are market-orientated, that is, they set out to make what the consumer wants at a price which will be sure to sell and make a profit. Makers of children's videos, for example, know that a new product must look good, be affordable, and have a new theme or characters to appeal to the age group. Market research ensures the product suits the market.

Consumers can be classified into different groups or 'market segments'. Advertising campaigns and pricing can be targeted at the group most likely to buy the product. A children's video will be wanted by children, but bought by parents, so they may put adverts in children's comics and on children's TV and also run high street poster campaigns.

Clever promotion can extend the sales of a product for long periods. Attractive packaging, links with popular places or celebrities and spin-off products are all techniques which can extend a product's life cycle. The packaging of a free toy character with a children's video, for instance, or special re-packaging of the video for Christmas, will keep the original product in the public eye.

The price of a product is a key factor. If it sounds right, the market share will be higher. £7.99 sounds much cheaper than just 1p off £8.00. A business must make the correct pricing decisions if it is to cover costs, make a profit and compete with rival products. Special deals or different price bands may prove useful.

There are limits on the success of marketing. No amount of packaging will sell a poor product in the longer term, and there are laws to prevent a business making false claims for their products (see page 79).

Market research - what does a business want to know?

A business already has information to hand on its past performance:

information on past performance:
- are sales up or down on last year?
- has our market share increased?
- have our profits increased?
- why did this product fail?
- which products did best?

information on future trends:
- can we keep sales going on existing products?
- can we launch a new product?
- which groups should we aim it at?
- what share of the market can we expect to win?
- are competitors planning new products?
- are there any new competitors?
- are there any new laws or technologies to consider?

?

It needs to research further to plan for the future.

information on current status:
- how much of the market share do we have?
- who is buying our products?
- why are they buying them?
- are our prices competitive?
- is advertising reaching the right people?
- are customers satisfied with quality?
- is someone else's product selling better?
- which of our products are selling better than others?

SWOT analysis

Businesses looking at their position in a market, and how to improve it, often use the **SWOT** approach:

Strengths and
Weaknesses
} Internal factors over which a business has some control, e.g. costs of overheads, materials and labour.

Opportunities and
Threats
} External factors over which a business has little or no control, e.g. the performance of a competitor, new government legislation.

ⓉⓋ Market research

Businesses collect and analyse information from and about customers in order to come up with a **marketing strategy** - a plan for gaining new customers, increasing sales, etc. The information they need comes from research.

You need to know:

■ the types of things a business needs to find out (see FactZONE, page 67)

■ how businesses analyse and divide the market

■ the differences between desk and field research

■ the different types of surveys and questions

> **❗ REMEMBER**
>
> Market research helps to reduce some of the risks in business.

Market segments

When trying to decide the best way to sell their product, businesses divide customers into different groups, or **market segments**, according to different characteristics. A business may want to know, for instance, which sex or age group is particularly keen on a product or service, for instance a new range of snacks, or a judo course at a leisure centre. This gives them a target for their advertising and packaging, and helps them refine the product.

The socio-economic market segments, used by government and many businesses, are based on characteristics of income, education and occupation:

Group A	Professionals	3%	Group C2	Skilled manual	33%
Group B	Management/technical	12%	Group D	Semi-skilled manual	20%
Group C1	Supervisory/clerical	22%	Group E	Unskilled manual	10%

Desk and field research

Research involves collecting and analysing information. It can be expensive and time-consuming. **Desk research** means working with existing material, such as published accounts of the performance of rivals, government reports and data from consumer groups, councils or marketing companies. Such data is called **secondary data**. Collecting and analysing information gained first-hand, via interviews and surveys, is called **field research**, and the data is **primary data.**

Primary data - original data
Up-to-date, directly relevant to products.
Targeted at customers of business.
Research methods and questions can be controlled by business and remain confidential.
Can be expensive.

Secondary data - published data
Wide range of general data available.
Quick to handle.
Usually free.
Can be out-of-date or off-target.

Surveys, questions and results

A business may choose one of a number of different types of survey, when looking for customer data. *Quantity* of response (data) needs to be weighed against *quality*.

- One-on-one surveys are generally either street or telephone questionnaires (good for quantity of data) or longer in-depth interviews (good for quality).
- Postal surveys are easy to set up, but have a low rate of return and low quality of data.
- Group surveys, where a panel of people are brought together to comment on a product, produce high quality, but low quantity, of data.

A survey may be:

- random, where each person (in a given area) has an equal chance of being asked.
- based on quotas, where a set number of people from each market segment are interviewed.
- targeted, where questions are only put to one particular market segment.

The questions could be:

- 'closed', where the interviewee has to choose from a set of possible answers, for instance multiple choice questions or 'scales', where preferences need to be shown by numbering a list with first choice, second choice, etc.
- 'open', with no pre-set answers.

Closed questions give answers that are easy to analyse, but provide limited data. Answers to open questions are more valuable, but harder to analyse.

Results

- Quantitative (measurable) information can easily be presented as graphs or charts (e.g. to show which groups are buying a product most).

- Qualitative information gives detail and depth, and data is often presented by businesses using particular examples or case studies (e.g. to explain why a product appeals to a particular type of person).

Practice question

A petrol station is planning to expand its payment area to include a small shop, offering a range of services and products to customers.

1. The petrol station manager may want to know the age range and occupation of the customers. List two other pieces of data about them which would be useful.

2. Explain why this sort of data is useful.

What might the manager be thinking of stocking? What would be useful data to help him decide (for instance, between car magazines and comics)?

🔲 The marketing mix

❗ REMEMBER

Each business is likely to have its own special marketing mix.

Having determined its marketing strategy, a business needs to apply the right **marketing mix** to carry it out successfully. This is the set of 'ingredients' that the business will use to achieve its aims, and is based on the 'four Ps' (see below). A successful marketing mix of a good product in the right place at the right price, with attractive packaging and advertising, wins customers and makes profits more likely. As the marketing strategy for a product, or range of products, progresses, it is likely to be changed and amended, depending on its success. Each change will involve a change in the marketing mix – more money and time will be spent on some 'P' elements, and less on others.

You need to know:

■ the 'four Ps' elements of marketing mix

■ how the 'four Ps' relate to marketing strategy

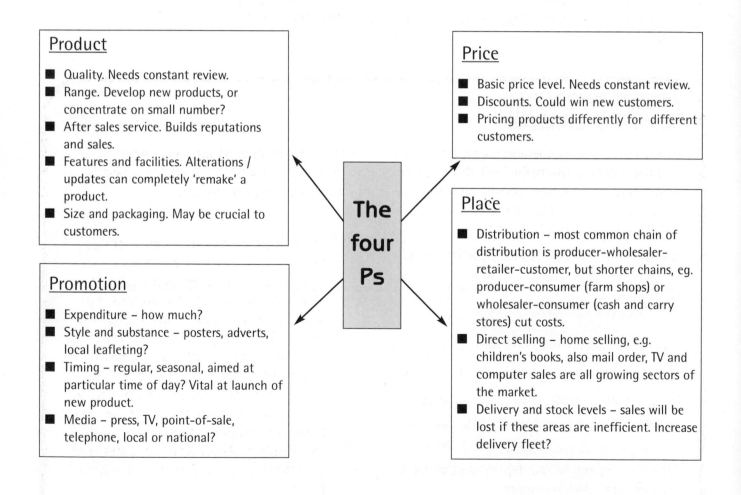

Product

■ Quality. Needs constant review.
■ Range. Develop new products, or concentrate on small number?
■ After sales service. Builds reputations and sales.
■ Features and facilities. Alterations / updates can completely 'remake' a product.
■ Size and packaging. May be crucial to customers.

Promotion

■ Expenditure – how much?
■ Style and substance – posters, adverts, local leafleting?
■ Timing – regular, seasonal, aimed at particular time of day? Vital at launch of new product.
■ Media – press, TV, point-of-sale, telephone, local or national?

The four Ps

Price

■ Basic price level. Needs constant review.
■ Discounts. Could win new customers.
■ Pricing products differently for different customers.

Place

■ Distribution – most common chain of distribution is producer-wholesaler-retailer-customer, but shorter chains, eg. producer-consumer (farm shops) or wholesaler-consumer (cash and carry stores) cut costs.
■ Direct selling – home selling, e.g. children's books, also mail order, TV and computer sales are all growing sectors of the market.
■ Delivery and stock levels – sales will be lost if these areas are inefficient. Increase delivery fleet?

Marketing strategy and marketing mix

In creating the marketing mix for a product or range of products, a business will concentrate on different elements from the lists opposite. For instance, if the marketing strategy is to establish a new product in an existing market, a company might decide to concentrate on low pricing and swift and efficient delivery. It may not have much money left for promotion (relying instead on word-of-mouth marketing). If a business is trying to boost the sales of a well-established product, on the other hand, its marketing mix may involve creating new product features and improving product quality, running a new advertising campaign, and trying to attract a new group of customers.

Different companies place different emphasis on elements of the marketing mix. One supermarket chain may base its place in the market on a continuing reputation for low prices, another on its reputation for quality, range of products and presentation.

◎ *A book business is changing the way in which it sells books. It is adding a site on the Internet to its traditional chain of shops in UK cities. What changes to the marketing mix do you think should be made to ensure success?*

Practice question

A fast food chain is opening a new restaurant in a town centre. Marketing efforts are going to be aimed at raising awareness amongst local people. The budget is £10 000, and various methods could be used:

Large posters on key sites ... ... £400 per poster
per month

Local leaflets ... ... £175 per 10,000
leaflets

Local paper adverts ... ... £550 per advert

Local schools competition ... £500 for prizes

Meal discount offers ... ... £2 per meal

Radio adverts ... ...£300 per
30 seconds

Future marketing would depend on the sales revenue from the restaurant.

1. What methods would you use to promote the fast food restaurant and why?

2. Once the restaurant was open, what marketing mix could be used to ensure customers kept returning?

(?) *Think about which approach might be best, but make sure your answer compares it with other approaches, to show you understand the options (e.g. a high profile but expensive poster and radio campaign over a month, compared to local, cheaper leaflets and discount offers over six months). Remember to give reasons for your choice. For part 2, bring in ideas of your own to show you know the meaning of marketing mix. You would probably want to target your customers very carefully. Can you think how?*

ⓣ The product life cycle

However brilliant a concept, a product unwanted by consumers will not sell. Other products may sell very well for a while and then lose their popularity. Firms spend large amounts of money on good research and product development before marketing their products, and on extending the life cycles of these products once they are in the market.

You need to know:

■ the different stages of a typical product life cycle

■ how product development takes place

■ how life cycles may be extended, and the importance of branding

Products have a natural life cycle which begins with their development and launch, moves through a period of growth to maturity and to a point where the market is full of similar competing products. Finally a loss of sales leads to the end of the cycle. This can all be shown on a graph, as shown below.

Hi-tech products such as computers tend to have a short life cycle, as new developments quickly make old machines outdated. Standard essentials, such as salt and soap, generally have very long cycles.

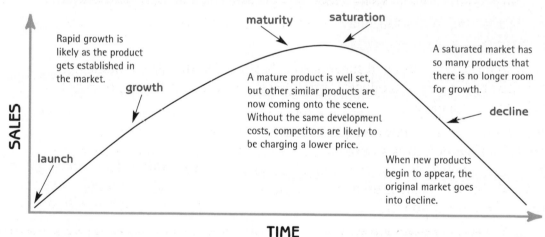

Rapid growth is likely as the product gets established in the market.

growth

launch

maturity   **saturation**

A mature product is well set, but other similar products are now coming onto the scene. Without the same development costs, competitors are likely to be charging a lower price.

A saturated market has so many products that there is no longer room for growth.

decline

When new products begin to appear, the original market goes into decline.

SALES

TIME

Product development

Forward-looking businesses are always looking to develop new and improved products. The main elements in product development are:

■ Establishing customer needs
■ Generating new ideas
■ Checking production is viable (e.g. whether raw materials are available) and whether the business can afford to go ahead (e.g. whether finance can be raised and whether they will break even)
■ Producing prototypes and testing them
■ Test marketing
■ Developing a marketing strategy.

Extending the life cycle

Businesses use many different methods to try and extend product life cycles. By changing strategy and altering the marketing mix (see pages 70-71), a great deal is possible. Below are some examples of how life cycles can be lengthened:

■ Extra advertising and promotion
■ New packaging (e.g. luxury versions, Christmas specials)
■ Special deals (buy one, get one free)
■ Widening the product range, e.g. a children's publisher might produce videos of books
■ Changing the product image to aim at a new market segment
■ Diversifying a product (e.g. Mars ice cream bar, Kit Kat orange flavour bar, Discovery version of the Land Rover). This is easier with strong branding
■ **Branding.** This involves developing a product's name with a distinctive logo, colours and packaging, and registering all this to prevent other companies copying it. Branding helps by:
 - making customers feel secure with regard to quality
 - making it hard for new rivals to gain attention
 - making it simpler for customers to choose

Strong branding is evident in the sweets market with some £126 million spent each year on advertising. It is possible to push a completely new brand into the 'top twenty' selling sweets within a year or two, but big sweet firms like Cadbury's have successfully maintained up to forty different brand versions of chocolate.

Many high-street stores and supermarkets have copied the idea of branding for their own range of products. 'Own brands' now account for one third of sales in supermarkets.

Branding may not work where products are seen as essentially the same by consumers. Fresh fruit is an example, although Outspan and others have had some success. Also, some brand names lose their impact altogether, as when a market leader's name is used by everyone to refer to all products in the market (e.g. biros, hoovers).

❗ REMEMBER

Fashions can repeat themselves. Yoyos have come back to life after decline on several occasions.

Practice question

Allsports manufacture high quality sports and leisure shoes. The shoes are made for specialist shops and department stores to sell under their own labels. Allsports are now thinking of marketing their own brand label of sports shoes in what is a very competitive market.

1. What is meant by 'a very competitive market'? Use examples to illustrate your answer.

2. What problems might *Allsports* have in marketing its own brand label?

⑦ *Think about the number of firms, products or the amount of advertising. In your answer, make sure you identify problems, but also link them to Allsports' business.*

ⓣ Pricing decisions

Prices of goods must be set to cover the cost of making them (see break-even point, page 37) and to allow some profit for the business, but pricing is also part of an overall marketing strategy aimed at persuading customers to buy your product rather than someone else's. Prices must be carefully monitored and adjusted as and when necessary to take account of such things as new competition, or rises and falls in demand. (See also marketing mix, pages 70-71.)

❗ REMEMBER

£2.00 is not a good price. £1.99 'feels' much lower.

You need to know:

■ the links between price, supply and demand in the market

■ different pricing policies used by firms

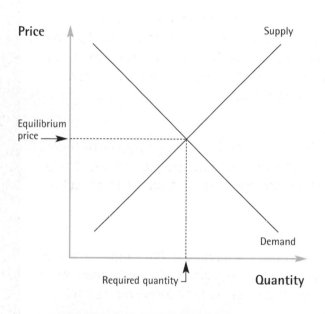

Price, supply and demand

In theory, the higher the price of a product, the more a business will supply. From the consumer's end, though, the higher the price, the less they will demand. The price at which the supply and demand curves meet (the equilibrium price) is the ideal price to set, as it will satisfy both a business and its customers and the market will 'clear'. Too low a price, and demand will outstrip supply. Too high a price and there will be a surplus of unsold products.

In practice, it is difficult to gather information about all the decisions of businesses and consumers, so businesses set prices based on their objectives and 'best guesses' about the state of the market. The different types of pricing policy they may adopt are shown in the FactZONE opposite.

Practice question

Fill-up Foods plc make and sell snacks in a very competitive market. Market research suggests a gap in the adult snacks market, but pricing will be important. The marketing manager suggested that prices could start low and could then rise to increase profitability once brand loyalty was established.

1. Explain what might happen to sales if *Fill-up's* price was higher than that charged by competitors.

2. Suggest and explain alternative pricing policies that the company might use.

❓ *Think about the links between prices and customer behaviour - you may want to suggest other things which might influence the customer's choice apart from price.*

Pricing policies

Cost-plus pricing

A very common approach to pricing. A business adds a percentage mark-up to the total unit costs (variable and fixed) of producing an item. This gives them their profit margin. It is a fairly crude approach, as it does not take into account such things as variations in fixed costs with output, or what customers are willing to pay. (A similar pricing policy, **contribution pricing**, sets prices to cover variable costs and make a contribution towards fixed costs.)

Competitive pricing

A policy whereby a firm sets its price close to those of competitors. In effect, competition then becomes a matter of non-price features such as the level of service or the extras included in the price.

Loss-leaders

A policy which sets prices at or below cost (with no mark-up) in order to penetrate a new market, for example, satellite TV companies giving away dishes in order to get subscribers for pay channels. Supermarkets often use this approach to attract customers to cheap goods on the basis that they will then buy other items. The term **penetration pricing** may be used for this policy, though it usually refers to pricing above cost but lower than rivals.

Skimming (or creaming) the market

A policy which takes advantage of the uniqueness of a new product, for instance a piece of high-tech equipment. It is given a very high price because a firm knows wealthy people will buy it as a luxury and high development costs can be recovered. Later, the price can be dropped to attract a different part of the market.

Price discrimination

A policy of charging different prices to different people for the same product. Rail companies and airlines use this widely. Train passengers, for instance, comprise a large range of people, some of whom have to travel at a set time and pay a premium for rush hour travel; others who can fill empty seats at a very low price at different times of day.

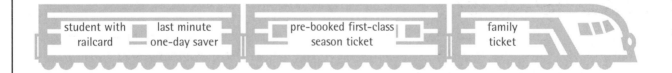

student with railcard | last minute one-day saver | pre-booked first-class season ticket | family ticket

Consumer-led pricing

Consumers develop a sense of a 'fair price', and products priced at rates too far above or below won't sell well, unless perceived as true 'luxury' or 'bargain' products. This is known as a 'price plateau' and all businesses must pay careful attention it.

⊞ Promoting products

Promotion is how a firm tells likely customers about a product and its benefits, in order to boost sales. It involves a mixture of information and persuasion and includes everything from advertising to free gifts. As part of its marketing strategy, a business may choose to spend more or less money on the promotion of a product at stages in its life cycle, in relation to money spent in other areas of its marketing mix (see pages 70-71).

You need to know:

■ the different types of promotion used by businesses

■ the different advertising methods used

■ the purpose of advertising

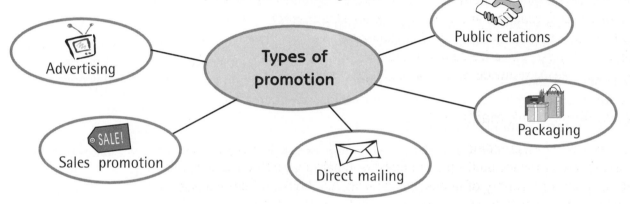

Advertising

Most companies use some form of advertising to promote their products. This can be through a variety of media, such as:

■ TV, radio and cinema
■ Newspapers and magazines
■ Journals or specialist publication
■ Posters on billboards

❗ REMEMBER
Bad advertising is controlled by the Advertising Standards Authority (see page 79)

Some types of advertising are more expensive than others, and are likely to reach many more people. A small local firm of plumbers will most likely advertise in a local paper at a cheap rate. Large multinational companies, such as car manufacturers, spend millions on expensive national TV campaigns designed and run by advertising agencies. Businesses spend over £12 billion on advertising in the UK. The largest part is spent on press and TV adverts.

Why advertise?

■ to persuade people to buy the product
■ to change people's attitudes
■ to make people think better of an organisation
■ to provide basic information

Public relations

Public relations aim to keep a company's name in the public eye and ensure good customer relations. A public relations department is responsible for:
■ press releases (e.g. about a new product)
■ organising sponsorships and awards (e.g. for sports or educational activities)
■ damage limitation - putting the company point of view in the event of unfavourable publicity

Sales promotion

Sales promotion activities, all aimed at boosting sales, include:
■ special offers (buy two, get one free)
■ price discounts
■ vouchers, coupons and customer loyalty cards (very successful for petrol stations, supermarkets and other large retailers)
■ joint promotion (where one firm links to another e.g. McDonalds and Disney, or washing machine and washing powder manufacturers)
■ point of sale materials (displays and packaging in store)
■ free gift campaigns or prize competitions (e.g. in children's book or toy shops, or through nationwide 'win a car'-type promotions)

Direct mailing ('junk mail')

Direct mailing involves sending promotional material to targeted customers, using databases of names built up from questionnaires, guarantee cards etc. It is used to promote a variety of goods and services, e.g. book and music clubs, financial services, charity work, photographic and printing services.

Packaging

A product is often defined by its packaging, which can be the most persuasive ingredient when consumers choose an item from the shelf. Good packaging must protect the product, be the right size and shape for easy use by distributors and customers, and must also have consumer appeal. Many large companies use professional design agencies to help them develop the most eye-catching look, and also to create seasonal looks, e.g. at Christmas.

Practice question

Look at the data on page 74 about *Fill-up Foods plc* and the snacks they hope to sell. They are aiming at pubs, supermarkets and garages. What might be the advantages and disadvantages of a local TV advert campaign as a way of promoting the new snack?

? *Think about the audience for such adverts, and the kind of image the snack should be given. Which other approaches might be considered?*

The business environment

This section is about:

- Business and competition
- Business and the community
- The national economy
- Business in Europe
- The global economy

A business has to make important decisions about organisation, finance, production and marketing. These internal decisions are important but the success of the business also depends on the performance of rival businesses, on good working relationships with the local community, and on the ups and downs of the national and international economy.

Factors in the business environment

If there was just one store selling computers and computer software, then a business could set a high price. When there are many competing businesses, the customer is likely to find lower prices, better service and lots of new products coming onto the market. The Government makes sure customers are not cheated by passing consumer protection laws.

Large out-of-town stores can offer lots of choice and cheaper prices to customers with cars. Local communities can benefit from bright new shopping malls. But there may be costs as well - old town centre shops can lose customers and traffic may increase. Government planning rules can help to control the balance between open countryside and built-up areas.

Sales of computers depend on good marketing by a business but also on customers with money to spend. If unemployment is rising and customers are saving for bad times ahead, then no business will find it easy to sell products. High interest rates can make it hard for businesses to borrow funds for new factories or to develop new products.

A UK computer software business selling its products to the home market is likely to face a lot of competition from foreign firms. The business may also wish to expand and sell abroad. Its prices may be lower than those of rival firms but a high UK exchange rate can make it hard to sell to other countries. Labour costs may be lower in other countries and a UK business may find it hard to compete.

Business and competition – laws and organisations

The UK Government and the European Union have passed laws to stop businesses getting together and fixing prices or restricting supplies.

In Britain, the Monopolies and Mergers Commission investigates any case where:
- 25% or more of the whole market is in one business's hands
- a merger between businesses involves assets worth more than £70 million.

The government can stop a merger or tell a business to change its anti-competitive behaviour.

Consumer laws

The three main laws protecting the consumer are:
- Trade Descriptions Act (1968 and 1972) . . . . . Stops businesses giving misleading information
- Consumer Credit Act 1974 . . . . Protection when borrowing or buying on credit
- Sale and Supply of Goods Act 1994 . . . . Products have to be of 'satisfactory quality'

Local government help

- Trading Standards Officers check on faulty products, and weights and measures (things such as scales, petrol pump measures etc).
- Environmental Health Officers check on such things as food hygiene, pollution and illegal waste disposal.
- An Ombudsman checks public complaints, e.g. against health and government services.

Independent organisations

- The British Standards Institute (BSI) tests products for safety and quality. It issues 'Kitemarks' to show that a product has met certain standards.
- Citizens Advice Bureaux provide free advice and help people to make complaints.
- The Office of Fair Trading provides information and advice leaflets. Its Director General is responsible for consumer law.
- OFTEL, OFGAS, OFWAT are agencies set up by the Government when certain industries were privatised (see page 17). They check that the private businesses don't take advantage of their monopoly position to charge high prices.

Voluntary codes

- Some industries have set up their own **codes of conduct**, which set standards for businesses in dealing with customers, e.g. the Association of British Travel Agents (ABTA) promises to get customers home from holiday if a firm goes bust.
- Advertisers are encouraged to make 'legal, decent, honest and truthful' adverts by the Advertising Standards Authority (ASA).

Business and competition

You need to know:

- how governments and other organisations protect businesses and consumers from unfair competition and bad practice (see FactZONE, page 79)
- what external influences there are on businesses
- what makes a competitive environment, and how firms should act, to do well
- why business activity needs to be controlled

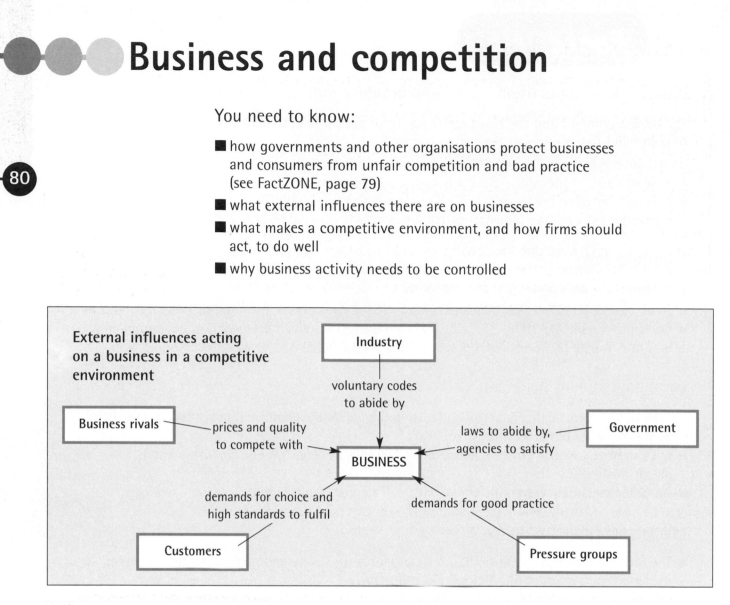

External influences acting on a business in a competitive environment

Industry — voluntary codes to abide by → BUSINESS

Business rivals — prices and quality to compete with → BUSINESS

Government — laws to abide by, agencies to satisfy → BUSINESS

Customers — demands for choice and high standards to fulfil → BUSINESS

Pressure groups — demands for good practice → BUSINESS

If a business is to survive in a competitive industry with lots of rival firms, then it must look both to win customers and pay close attention to their needs.

Businesses are trying to win customers in what are often very competitive environments, for instance:

- where there are many rival businesses (e.g. town centre clothes shops)
- where there are a few very large rivals with keenly-priced goods (large food supermarkets)
- where customers have a wide choice of products (restaurants)
- where new technology is constantly leading to new products (mobile phone businesses)

A business which gives good personal service and has a good reputation for replacing faulty products will generally do well, but other aspects to consider are: good marketing techniques (see pages 66-77), competitive pricing, high levels of quality and standards, and good response to issues that may be raised by pressure groups. Businesses that cut corners in an effort to win customers may find themselves with a bad reputation that is hard to shrug off.

! REMEMBER Competition can encourage businesses to keep down costs, but it can also lead to wasteful advertising and bad practice.

Why businesses need controls

- Fierce competition can lead businesses to make exaggerated claims for their products.
- A very successful firm can charge ridiculously low prices to force rivals out of business.
- When one firm dominates the market, it does not have to worry about customer views.
- Some products may be profitable but also undesirable (cigarettes, alcohol).

Laws and voluntary codes can make sure that businesses pass on accurate information to customers, and they can be taken to court for bad practice. Agencies like the Trading Standards Office and the Environmental Health Office investigate local complaints and prosecute offending businesses. At a national and European level, businesses with large shares of a market can be reported if they try to overcharge customers or squeeze rivals out of business unfairly. Pressure groups can use publicity to make life very awkward for businesses practices they see as offensive.

Consumer entitlements

If goods are faulty or don't do what's claimed, you can have them replaced or receive a refund. The retailer is responsible for meeting your claim, not the manufacturer.

Trade associations, which represent an industry, will help you handle any complaints about their members. As a last resort, you can take the retailer to the **small claims court** where the process is kept simple.

Car firms want your advice on a voluntary code for advertising. Can you think of examples of bad practice which you feel should be forbidden by the code?

Practice question

Baz puts some T-shirts on sale at a reduced price in his clothes shop. He labels each one with a note to say that it has faded after being on display in the window. A customer buys a T-shirt but returns next day saying she wants her money back.

a) Explain whether the customer is justified in her complaint. Refer to any relevant consumer protection laws.

b) State and explain one action Baz could take.

c) Suggest two organisations that the consumer could go to for advice.

d) What actions could these organisations take if the law had been broken?

Is there anything Baz must do? Is there anything he could do to encourage the customer to return again? For part d, remember some organisations can take legal action, some can offer advice.

Business and the community

Businesses need to have good working relationships with their local community if they are to continue to operate in the long term. Some costs and benefits of business activities may be experienced by the wider community as well as by the business and its customers.

You need to know:

■ the meaning of external costs and benefits of business activity
■ what can be done about external costs

❗ REMEMBER

When businesses refer to costs, they usually leave out costs to the community such as pollution or congestion caused by their activities.

The profit and loss account, and pricing levels, of a business are a reflection of its internal costs and benefits. But there are also some external costs and benefits, which are felt by the community beyond the business. External benefits add to the welfare of the community, but external costs cause problems. It can be difficult to get anyone to take responsibility for damage and difficult to put an accurate figure on the cost.

To have a medium-sized business set up or expand in an area:

External benefits may include:
Improved transport and communications. New roads, play areas etc.
Job gains. New employment and income.
Extra spending in local shops from those employed.
Regeneration of local area, new buildings, shops etc., because of new wealth.
Efficient recycling - some businesses can use the heat from waste burners as a power source.

External costs may include:
Pollution. Noise and smell from factories and traffic.
Safety hazards from factories and traffic.
Waste products for disposal (general rubbish, also smoke, gases, toxic substances).
Building in rural areas. Damage to beauty spots and wildlife populations.
Job losses. Unemployment from failure and closure of rival businesses.
Lost income and spending power of those unemployed.
Loss of local services. Useful local buildings and services may have to be closed to make way for developments.

◎ *A new proposal for an out-of-town shopping centre might attract support from those who see more shops, jobs and a better image for the local community.*

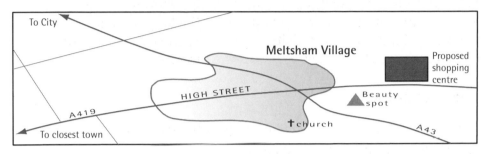

What might those people who are opposed to the proposal see as potential costs?

A business and its local community should look to balance external costs and benefits, to arrive at a solution satisfactory to all. It can be difficult to put an actual figure on external costs and to persuade customers or business owners to pay for them (although some businesses, such as Body Shop and BP have begun to include costs of their activities to local communities in their balance sheets). However, if costs are looked at in terms of offsetting benefits, agreements may be reached.

For example:

■ Some businesses have replaced production techniques with versions that are more environmentally friendly (an external benefit), but customers have agreed to pay more for the products in return.

■ A community charges a company high business rates (local tax), but in return pays for the up-keep of the road, and the refuse-collection service, to its out-of-town site.

■ The Government has begun to think about 'green taxes' to pay for external environmental costs – for example, charging businesses for the cost of maintaining roads used by fleets of lorries. A high licence fee can be charged for each lorry.

Practice question

A large new leisure theme park is proposed for an area outside a small town. A major road passes through the centre of the town and some people have long argued for a by-pass.

1. List some of the possible external benefits which the theme park might bring for the local community.

2. What might be some of the external costs?

3. How could these be paid for if the development went ahead?

⑦ *There will be some immediate and some longer-term benefits. Think about how different elements of the local community might be affected. The customers of the leisure park will pay to get in. How might this money be used?*

The national economy

The activities of a business may be affected by government policies and by the state of the national economy in general. Businesses expect governments to steer the economy towards steady growth and to avoid big changes in prices, interest rates and exchange rates.

You need to know:

■ what is meant by government policy
■ how changes in policies can affect businesses
■ how business is affected by booms and slumps in the economy

Governments play a part in all world economies, though some take a more active part in business activity than others. In the UK, we expect our government to make sure businesses operate fairly (see page 79), but also:

■ to provide some goods and services for everyone (see pages 16-17 on the public sector)
■ to ensure the poorest are helped by the better-off (through taxes and benefits)
■ to keep price levels steady and to encourage training and jobs

The government taxes income, spending and business profits, and uses the money for welfare benefits, services like health and education, and investment in new roads and buildings (some of these spending and support policies are specifically targeted at the poorer regions of the country). This **fiscal policy** is managed through the yearly **Budget.**

The government also makes changes in interest rates (**monetary policy**) to encourage borrowing and investment by consumers and businesses.

> **! REMEMBER**
>
> Taxes are collected from workers and consumers to pay for government activity, but most people also benefit from government spending on welfare and other services.

Practice question

Read the FactZONE opposite, but then cover it before you try this question.

A Canadian Company, Carco, has decided to set up a new factory in the UK, in Kirston, a town that has suffered a decline since the closure of a major industrial plant. The local council has been working hard to improve roads and to subsidise a new industrial estate, which has been designated as an Enterprise Zone.

1. Kirston Business Park is an Enterprise zone. What does this mean to *Carco*?

2. How else does *Carco* benefit from setting up in Kirston?

3. Why is the arrival of *Carco* important for the region and for the economy?

② *Think about the advantages to be gained by a company setting up in such an area, and also about the effects of the company's arrival on other businesses.*

FactZONE

Taxes and their effects

Income tax

The UK government takes 30-35% of pay through income tax and national insurance contributions. Currently, the basic rate of income tax is 25% for most workers. A higher tax rate leaves people with less income and so discourages spending. It may also reduce the hours people are willing to work.

Value Added Tax (VAT)

A tax on spending (17.5% on many goods and services excluding essential items like children's clothes and basic food). Higher taxes discourage spending and may also push up overall prices.

Corporation tax

Tax paid by companies on their income (profit). A rise in this tax could mean less investment and cuts in future employment levels.

What does the government do with the money taken in taxes?

The money pays for education, health and other services as well as a wide range of welfare benefits. But it also helps businesses through a variety of schemes:

- Assisted areas: grants are given to businesses who set up within the designated area.
- Inner cities: development corporations take over a whole area that has declined, rebuild the infrastructure of roads, leisure facilities, public transport, etc, and oversee the private sector's investment in the area.
- Enterprise zones: business spending on new buildings is not taxed in these areas and businesses do not have to pay business rates for a period of time.
- Small businesses: get help with loans and start-ups.

The European Union also provides grants and has enterprise zone schemes.

Managing the business cycle

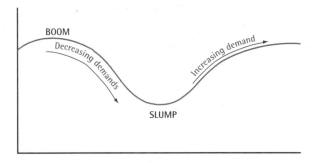

Growth in UK business output averages 2-3% a year but it tends to fluctuate in cycles every 4-5 years. Growth and employment are helped by high demand in the economy. If demand outstrips supply, there can be a general increase in prices (inflation) and business planning becomes very difficult. If the government raises taxes and interest rates, it can reduce demand but at the risk of pushing up unemployment and shaking the confidence of businesses.

Rising prices affect:

Jobs: fewer goods bought by consumers, falling sales, cut back on employment.

Trade: UK goods prices rise faster than those of foreign competitors; exports fall, imports rise.

Business costs: prices of raw materials up, workers want more pay to cover higher prices; upward pressure on business costs.

Business and Europe

UK businesses now operate in a European Union shared by 15 countries with a market of some 370 million people. The EU has regulations, policies and guidelines which help and control business activity. Over 51% of the UK's overseas trade is with other EU countries, making the EU of great importance.

You need to know:

■ the main features of the EU
■ how EU membership, and EU developments, affect businesses
■ the advantages and disadvantages of the single currency

❗ REMEMBER

There are many different perspectives on Europe. Don't forget to write about how EU membership benefits business.

The EU has set out to achieve social and economic progress for its members through economic growth and expansion of trade. The EU Budget is financed by contributions from member governments and from tariffs (taxes charged) on imports from outside the EU.

■ People can seek jobs throughout the EU.

■ People and goods can travel freely across member countries. The EU is a single market - its members pay no tariffs (taxes) to move goods from country to country (so there are also no border delays which might further increase costs).

■ VAT (see page 85) has been harmonised - it cannot fall below 15% in any EU country. Attempts to bring other taxes into line have led to difficulties with businesses such as ferry companies who benefit from tax-free sales.

■ The Social Chapter sets out rights and regulations for the workplace - such things as hours of work, pension rights, etc, as well as health and safety matters. Small businesses in the UK have found these rules tough to meet, and they may increase costs.

■ Major help is provided for the poorer regions, which include part of the UK.

■ Consumer laws protect consumer rights throughout the whole of the EU, and free competition between businesses is upheld. The EU investigates any merger between businesses with interests in two or more EU countries, and sets rules on subsidies given to businesses.

■ The Common Agricultural Policy helps create security for farmers by buying produce at guaranteed prices (farmers' profits and business survival is risky because of weather fluctuations and market uncertainties). If the real market prices are low, this set price policy is very expensive for EU members (up to 70% of the entire EU budget), and it has also led to large surpluses when supply has outstripped demand.

■ The EU also provides grants to modernise farms.

■ The Common Fisheries Policy sets controls for the fishing industry. The EU sets the amount of fish that any country and any individual fisherman can catch. Each country has exclusive rights to fish its own coastal waters up to a six mile limit, with a further six miles of fishing area granted to it where some other countries may be allowed restricted fishing rights.

■ Environmental standards are set for all members. EU laws in this area are often stricter than British laws, especially on car exhaust pollution and the disposal of poisonous and harmful waste.

The single currency

From 1999, the **Euro** has become the single currency for the majority of EU member countries. A European central bank supports the system and each country has to keep its economy under strict control. The UK has not yet joined in with the single currency.

Advantages

✓

Businesses no longer have to pay a fee to change their money when selling or buying from other countries.

Businesses no longer have to worry about exchange rate fluctuations when trading across Europe.

The European Central Bank can make long term decisions for the benefit of the whole of Europe.

Disadvantages

✗

Individual countries lose direct control over their money. A decision which benefits Europe may not be good for an individual country.

Each country's economy has to be managed inside tight guidelines. This might cost too much in terms of unemployment, extra taxes and fewer choices for the government.

❗ REMEMBER

The UK economy has to be performing well compared with other EU countries if the UK is to benefit from joining the single currency.

Practice question

One of the best-known features of the EU is that there is a single market.

1. What is meant by a single market?

2. How does a single market help member countries trade in the EU?

3. Why is the single market helpful in persuading foreign firms to set up factories in the EU?

❓ *Think of EU as if it were a set of regions in the UK. What encourages trade across the regions? Without a single market, what would a Japanese car company have to consider before setting up?*

The global economy

Firms selling goods abroad have to compete in worldwide markets, but doing so successfully gives a country the revenue to buy specialist or cheap goods from abroad. UK traders face heavy competition in the world market place, but buy many raw materials and supplies from overseas and sell many goods abroad. Trading abroad means exchanging currencies, so any changes in the value of the pound affects British firms.

You need to know:

- the meaning of imports, exports and exchange rates
- how international trade brings benefits and problems for businesses
- how governments can help to protect businesses

International trade means:

✓ larger markets, with more opportunities for better sales and lower costs, consumers with a greater variety of tastes.

But it also means:

✗ greater distances for deliveries, customs taxes, paperwork and delay at international borders, the need for different currencies, promotional materials in other languages, different laws and customs to deal with.

Imports and exports

REMEMBER
Success at international trade depends not only on businesses setting competitive prices, but also on the exchange rate of the currencies.

Imports are goods and services bought from abroad with payments flowing out to foreign producers. UK producers sell **exports** abroad and the money earned comes back into the UK. The flows of money are recorded on the country's balance of payments.

Exchange rates

The value of the UK pound against other currencies is called its **exchange rate.** Foreign businesses need to exchange their currency for pounds in order to buy British goods, and foreign investors need to buy pounds if they want to invest in British companies. High interest rates in the UK can attract such foreign investors. As in any other market, an increase in demand for pounds pushes up the 'price' of the pound to a foreign buyer. This change in the exchange rate changes the price of exports and imports. Governments try to help trade by keeping the exchange rate as stable as possible.

At an exchange rate of £1 = DM4, a German company pay DM400 for £100-worth of UK materials.
If the exchange rate rose to £1 = DM5, the same goods would now cost DM500. UK exports would fall if buyers could buy more cheaply elsewhere.

The UK usually imports more than it exports. The country has a surplus on trade in services, but a big deficit on trade in goods means there is an overall **trade deficit**. To improve the situation, businesses need to make goods and services more competitive, for instance by investing in training and new technology. There are also a number of government measures used to try and solve the problem of a trade deficit:

■ Tariffs (taxes) on imports. This increases their price and encourages buyers to consider buying in their home market.

■ No taxes on exports. This encourages businesses seeking to be competitive in overseas markets.

■ Advice to businesses on selling in overseas markets.

■ Import quotas. This is where a country only allows a set number of imports into the country. Such a policy may lead to retaliatory bans on goods from that country.

■ Subsidies. A government gives money to its businesses to help keep down their costs and so enable them to charge lower prices than other countries.

■ Exchange control. A government may restrict access to foreign currency, which makes importing and travel more difficult.

■ Governments may mount an advertising campaign at home to encourage the buying of goods and services from the home market rather than foreign competitors, and also run trade fairs abroad to try and boost the image of their goods and services.

REMEMBER

Governments need to work together to encourage trade. A big tax put on imports by one country is likely to lead to retaliation from other countries.

◎ *Which of the above measures for solving trade deficits are these actions examples of?*

1. Firms exporting goods do not have to pay VAT.
2. Prince Charles appears at an exhibition of UK goods in Japan
3. 200 licences are available to non-EU firms to sell cutlery in the UK

Practice question

Jo runs a craft centre and restaurant near a well-known tourist attraction in Yorkshire. She expects trade from foreign tourists, especially the Japanese, to increase by 10% in the next six months and by up to 30% in the next year. She is thinking of extending her restaurant.

1. How might Jo's business be affected by

   a) a decrease in the value of the pound against the yen?

b) a slump in the Japanese economy?

2. What could the government do to help Jo's business in the long term?

⑦ *Think about the cost of a visit to Britain for Japanese visitors. Which way should the pound move against the yen to help Jo? Could the government give Jo any greater security?*

In pairs

Answer notes

The following pages contain a guide to the information you need to include in your answers to the practice questions and other tasks in the book. It is given in note form and only gives an outline, or suggested examples, of what your answers should contain. In an exam, the different lengths of questions on your question paper, and in some cases the stated number of marks allocated to each, will help you decide how much you need to write for each one.

Page 11 Practice question

1a) There is no limit on John Taylor's responsibility for debts if his business folds. He would lose the £5000, plus any other possessions he and his wife own.

1b) A legal sharing of the business decisions, liabilities and profits.

2a) Trader keeps all profits, takes all decisions, keeps control of product quality.

2b) Not enough finance to meet cash flow problems; ignorance/lack of skill in some key business activities; not enough money for good marketing.

Page 13 Practice question

1a) Limited (as in private limited company).

1b) Raises money through shares, shares only available to owners' family/close associates.

1c) Any one person's losses limited to amount put into the business by that person.

1d) The family would want to keep control of decisions. In a plc, shares can be bought by anyone through the share market. The family could be outvoted.

Page 15

a) Less risk, help and training available (few well-known brands in fruit produce).

b) Established product, successful brand image (branding is common in fast foods).

c) National marketing, help and training available (good publicity and technical knowledge are very important in the mobile phone market).

Page 15 Practice question

1) The national company has a well-known name and marketing support to offer.

2) Probably an annual fee or a share of any profits; costs of developing the product to fit in with the national company's specifications/image; costs of training to work within the company's system.

Page 16

Advantages: easier to raise finance with shareholders, possible lower prices for customers as costs could be cut, taxpayers wouldn't have to support the P.O.

Disadvantages: non-profitable services might be cut, quality of service might fall, not everyone would be able to afford essential services if they are now priced, co-ordination of services under one roof might end.

Page 17 Practice question

1) Moving ownership to the private sector by selling shares.

2a) Industry, e.g. BT, might have to put more emphasis on making profits to please shareholders.

2b) It has to meet customer needs, and this might mean widening the range of products and services on sale. It could also raise its own money now through loans and shares and so improve products through new investment.

2c) It may have to match products and prices of rival firms. Prices might come down or it might choose to specialise in certain products or services.

Page 19

Your chart is likely to have the governors and head at the top, followed by deputies, one of whom will have year heads and form tutors underneath for pastoral work, another will have the subject heads and their department teachers below them. (Most teachers will be part of both organisational groups in practice.) A head of English is likely to be in charge of a number of specialist teachers.
A teacher in charge of IT might work entirely alone, or might work across the board with all teachers who use IT.

Page 19 Practice question

1) Vanessa will be at the top of your chart. The others will share the next level.

2) The job is divided up into tasks so that each worker becomes a

specialist in a limited range of tasks, or just one task.

3) Human resources, marketing, logistics.

4) Chain of command: the number of levels in an organisation that are controlled.

Span of control: the number of people or processes controlled at a given level.

5) Controlling accounts, making payments.

6) Advantages: clear lines of responsibility, clear channels of communication.

Disadvantages: possible slow communication through lots of levels, lack of motivation in people at lower levels with little responsibility.

Page 21

A small charity shop is run with volunteer staff to keep costs down and raise as much money as possible for the charity. Its objectives may include educating customers as well as selling goods for profit and collecting donations. An independent greengrocer is likely to be in business for personal gain and for the pleasure of being in charge. The owner will look to respond to the needs of local customers as a priority.

Page 21 Practice question

1) Managers might have a more important role if sales increase. More sales may mean more profit.

2) Shareholders will probably receive higher annual dividends if sales are high.

3) Expansion should make it easier for customers in the south to get the clothes. Customers in the north might find that deliveries

are held up because the company is having to deal with more people and a wider distribution network.

4) Managers might offer shares of higher future profits as an incentive.

Page 25

You would want an agreement fixing: a regular daily/weekly supply of new releases and prizes, set prices for a given period, a quality level that all products must meet, penalties for late deliveries and a set payment date for materials.

Page 25 Practice question

1) Large scale production methods, applied to batches of different, but similar products - in this instance batches of clothes of different designs or colours.

2) Production processes can be repeated, using machines that can be switched easily to cope with different kinds of materials or designs. Costs are kept down but customers will still have a wide choice of products. Hand-made production may produce higher quality, unique clothes, but at too high a cost to sell easily in high street stores.

Page 26 Practice question

1. and 2. Automation - production processes done by machine, e.g. products such as paving stones and bags of fertiliser being stored and handled by robot trucks. CAM - computer-aided manufacturing, e.g. stock control linked to sales by computer. Computer control systems - automatic handling of basic day-to-day procedures, e.g. venting and watering of

greenhouses.

3. When most of production costs are spent on machinery rather than on staff. Staffing costs in the greenhouses will fall compared to costs of machinery when much of the care of plants were taken over by computer control systems.

4. In the short-term, redundancies due to machines taking work away from people. Long-term effects might include new but different jobs being created as the garden centre widens its range of products and services.

Page 29

Everyone in the factory should be looking out for faulty goods. All biscuits at the end should be good quality. The workers should be trained in quality techniques. There may be suggestion boxes around the factory and meetings advertised.

Page 29 Practice question

1. The move is a good idea from the management side if there are savings to be made by putting all the workers on one site, for instance if the costs of adapting the one site for everyone to fit in are less than the savings in transport costs between the two sites. A good idea from the workers' angle so long as jobs are not lost, or travel not greatly increased.

2a) Processes to ensure there are the fewest possible faults, e.g. testing the quality of a sample of plastic bowls at regular intervals throughout the factory.

2b) The computer control of the moulding process should ensure high quality - a similar approach could be taken to the addressing and checking on delivery of products to customers. The assembly and packaging supervisor could be given a specific set of things to look out for. A Kaizen approach would encourage all workers to look for faults or suggest improvements. Good quality pay and bonuses would help to motivate staff.

⟨?⟩ Page 31

Arguments for: more jobs for locals, profits could bring other benefits to the area.

Arguments against: jobs might have to go to outside specialists, bulk of profits would go to shareholders, pollution risk high.

Page 31 Practice question

1. (i) Easy access for customers, (ii) local workers with right skills, (iii) good climate for outdoor pursuits.

2. Reasons for order as given in 1. above are: (i) large number of right kind of customers is essential for a "people" business, (ii) large number of workers important in most leisure businesses, local workers cheaper and a more stable workforce, (iii) good weather encourages customers generally (though not clear how much of this theme park is outdoors).

Page 34

Start-up: bread-slicing machine, computer, cleaning equipment, delivery van, staff training

Running costs: electricity, rent, sandwich fillings, wages

Renewal costs: repairs to van, replacement equipment

Page 35 Practice questions

1. Business plan should include a

cash flow forecast showing start-up, running and renewal costs, with sales/revenue estimates and a break-even prediction. The bank manager would want to know about 'collateral', i.e. assets of the group which could be used to raise money to repay the loan if the original £5000 was lost. There would need to be an agreement on the time period of the loan and the interest to be charged.

2a. Loans, grants or capital investment - major spending for a long period which should generate larger profits in the future.

2b. Leasing or retained profits - spread costs over a period of time without having to borrow serious amounts of money. Profits should be available if the business has been going some time.

2c. Leasing - probably best arrangement because it may not be a permanent need.

⟨?⟩ Page 38

Cut costs, e.g. find a cheaper supplier, reduce opening hours, cut wages. Raise prices or increase advertising to win more customers. If necessary, borrow money until business picks up.

Page 38 Practice question

1. Fixed cost examples - rent, electricity. Variable costs - bread, sandwich fillings.

2. When total costs are just covered by total (sales) revenue.

3. 1000 boxes per month. (Each sale covers the £1 variable cost of producing it, and raises £1 to go towards fixed costs).

4. So they know how many sales to aim at in order to run into profit.

5a) Break even sales now need to

be doubled - they must sell 2000 boxes.

5b) £1.40 per sale now goes towards fixed costs, so break-even level of sales falls to 715 boxes.

5c) Break-even sales figure rises to 1200 - they need to sell that many boxes per month.

⟨?⟩ Page 40

Lender wants to get a good idea of how well the business owner has thought through the finances ahead.

Unexpected costs are likely to crop up early in business. A planned overdraft will normally have an agreed, lower interest rate charge than an emergency one arranged in a hurry.

⟨?⟩ Page 41

A past cash flow forecast will tell you whether the owners had expected (and budgeted for) the losses. The figures can also be used to see how realistic are the plans for the next 6 months. If the losses have been expected, and a break-even point is planned within 12 months, then the business is probably OK.

Page 41 Practice question

1) Business was predicted to pick up sharply after a couple of bad months. It looks like this predicted increase in sales is linked to Christmas.

2) Sales were not so successful at Christmas (though there may have been some variation in costs, the cash situation is probably linked to sales). They have also fallen away quicker than expected.

3) and 4) If there is no great increase in sales over the summer,

then the business is
in trouble. They need to look
at ways of cutting costs or
boosting sales. There may have
been some unusually high costs in
the 6 months shown, so it
is important to compare the
figures with those from earlier
months, or those of similar
businesses.

② Page 44

The amount of working capital
available (as shown on the balance
sheet) will show if debts can be
repaid. The profit and loss account,
especially the figure for retained
profit, will guide decisions on
expansion.

Page 44 Practice question

1. Working capital = current assets
(£100,000) - current liabilities
(£75,000) = £25,000.

Capital employed (£165,000)
= share capital (£50,000) +
retained profit (£60,000) + loans,
so loans = £55,000

2. Fixed assets: factory, equipment,
machines. Current liabilities:
money owing to suppliers, short-
term loans owing to a bank.

3. Snapshot showing total
financial health of a business
at a particular time.

4. Record of money flows in and
out of a business over a time
period (usually a year). Allows
a comparison to be made with
business performance of other
years.

Page 46

To see that space, materials,
production processes etc. are
operating as efficiently as possible,
and to ensure that demand can be
met from current production and
stocks. Gross profit margins show
roughly how profitable the
business is in relation to its sales -
they are a crude measure of
success.

Page 46 Practice question

1. Current ratio = current assets :
current liabilities = 4000 :
800 = 5 : 1

2. The company has 5 times the
cash needed to cover its debts. This
is a very high figure and suggests
the company could be putting
more of its assets to work, e.g. by
expanding production.

Page 50 Practice question

When designing jobs: need to
think about skills of people
available, which tasks will interest
and motivate workers, which tasks
could be combined with machines
to keep costs down.

Staff could be rewarded through:
good basic pay and bonuses, good
working conditions, schemes which
make them feel part of the
business, e.g. profit sharing.

◎ Page 51

Cleaner: time rate + bonus. Fair
rate based on amount cleaned,
also opportunity to work quickly
to earn more.

Phone salesman: performance-
related pay, provided it is possible
to agree on what counts as good
performance.

Nurse: salary. Ensures good quality
work, not rushed, attention to
good care.

PO clerk: wage + overtime. Allows
employer to vary times
to suit busy periods.

Lorry driver: wage/salary. To
encourage good, safe driving and
delivery.

Page 51 Practice question

Some staff may be in a position to
benefit from extra hard, quick
work, rewarded by bonuses.
They would not be happy and may
leave. There may be no way, other
than training, for some workers to
improve their skills and therefore
their promotion chances. These
workers would also be unhappy.
On the other hand, workers who
feel undervalued may work better
as a result of a general increase in
hourly rates.

② Page 52

No need for consultation to draw
up job description and person
specification - only one manager
involved. May be no need for a
formal job contract
if the position is just a junior
assistant. Probably the only
training will be on the job - just
general guidance. References may
not be sought depending on
previous experience.

Page 54-55 Practice question

1. Probably Karen because her
qualifications fit the specification.
She also shows a lot of interest in
computing so she should learn
quickly. Paula does have
experience of retailing and she
may have proven skills with
handling money. You may choose
to interview her as well.

2. You could ask about the
candidate's shop experience, their
trustworthiness and reliability,
their ambitions to stay with the
company, their working knowledge
of computers and software, their
interests, their experience of

dealing with the public.

3. When a job vacancy is only advertised within a company, in order to recruit someone already employed by that company. The company need not spend money on external advertisement and management will be already aware of the skills and weaknesses of existing staff.

 Page 56

Bear in mind benefits can be either to the worker, the company or both. Also, the on-the-job training costs and benefits shown here can be "mirrored" to come up with those of off-the job training. On-the-job benefits (examples): no time lost in travel, the information is directly related to the work, workers are paid while training. Costs: the training may not be recognised as such by other companies, the area of training may be very specific and limited, there may be costs involved in setting up and running the training.

Page 56 Practice question

Off-the-job training will be designed specifically for this software package and will probably be of better quality than the company could provide itself. Though an off-the-job course would cost money, the company would otherwise have to train up its own specialist, which would take time (and therefore money). Such training would not be good value if it all has to be repeated when new software appears.

Page 57

Better quality workers in the long term who may stay longer with the company. This can save the costs of recruiting and training new workers.

Page 58

Plane ticket: the travel agent clearly has no way of checking the details of the phone message. It needs a better external system of confirming the booking at an earlier date. Complicated order form: again, poor external paperwork and no obvious customer relations dept. which could help the customer sort out the problem. Boss/supervisor: poor internal communications (formal and informal), with those in charge needing a much clearer idea of responsibilities.

Page 59 Practice question

Memo: note to personal assistant or fellow manager, i.e. a situation where good working relationships exist. Wrong to use where formal reports or copies are needed. Formal report: tabling a business proposal to the board. Wrong for telling something personal to employees. Circular letter: passing on less urgent news to a large number of people. Wrong to use where personal information is involved. Personal meeting: dealing with a personal issue, e.g. a promotion or a difficult matter. Wrong to use when a large number of people need to share decisions.

Page 60

Your report, in layout style, should include information to the effect that: IT makes it easier to communicate wherever employers/employees are based, better quality paperwork can be produced, most workers acquire better skills for presenting work more efficiently, more immediate contact with customers is made possible.

Page 60 Practice question

Example: publishing company uses teleworkers to edit material. Employer: saves costs of offices, workers need only be employed when needed, materials are easily exchanged between workers....but difficult to share creative ideas or to run conferences/meetings. Employees: work from home saves travel time, possible to fit work around other tasks, e.g. looking after children, can have home based anywhere, without needing to be close to an office....but may feel isolated and without support from fellow workers, pay rates may be lower, unseen costs may mount up at home, may be difficult to manage time effectively.

Page 61

All might agree on eventual introduction of new machinery with some training for those who volunteer (extra wages of 2%), and a 5% wage increase for everyone but linked to productivity. Employers might accept: longer time scale to introduce new machinery and training. Higher wage increases but higher productivity in return. Skilled workers: smaller wage increase but special role maintained, linked to new machinery. Unskilled workers: smaller increase and higher productivity expected.

Page 63 Practice questions

1. An overtime ban would make it harder for the firm to meet extra orders during busy periods. b) A work to rule takes away flexibility - if someone is away, then others will not do the work. It slows production down. c) If the firm has no stocks of chocolate, then sales will be lost while the strike is on. However, there will be no wages to pay, so costs will be down. If the strike goes on for some time, customers might switch to other brands, and be difficult to attract back later.

2. A Single Union agreement means that only one set of talks needs to take place. Workers have a stronger voice and managers have a simpler communications task.

Page 64 Practice question

1. She is hoping to increase the time during which customers can get telephone advice. She wants different workers to work different shifts.

2. Higher pay and decent equipment for home working.

3. Kim might not renew workers' contracts for the future. The union might threaten a work to rule or even a strike.

4. The main advice might be to slow down the pace of change and provide training to ensure workers accept, and are confident with, the new conditions. It might depend on how fast rival companies are changing.

Page 69 Practice question

1. How much customers usually spend in the shop, and what items they would wish the shop to stock.

2. It gives the manager a good idea of which goods to stock, and some idea of expected cash flow from the shop.

◎ Page 71

The business will need to advertise the service on other linked websites and in existing bookshops, as well as in magazines and papers. Prices might be reduced if the website selling process is predicted to be cheaper per book. A wider choice of books might be able to be offered on the website than in bookshops. The distribution centre may need to have a separate department devoted to meeting website customers' orders quickly.

Page 71 Practice question

1. You might choose local leaflets and posters because the main target is local customers. Meal discount offers might attract customers to start with.

2. A campaign which kept the restaurant in the customers' minds, e.g. local radio adverts and posters. A schools competition, and other types of school involvement would help if the main customer base is a young one, as would price reductions and special offers.

Page 73 Practice question

1. Lots of rival firms or rival products, as with sports products in general, also confectionery, cars, tools, photographic products, etc. Customers can be persuaded to buy a new product by a small change in price, a good advertising campaign or by strong branding. A change in colour of a brand leader's trainers may be enough to top the sales every year.

2. Loyalty to other brands might make it hard to persuade customers to switch. It might be hard to come up with an original brand idea. Since Allsports have been selling under shops' own labels, they have no reputation to build upon.

Page 74 Practice question

1. Unless the new product is something really special, customers will not buy it.

2. The business could go for a different product altogether, for example, a luxury snack deliberately targeted at wealthier customers. Prices could start high and be backed up by a glossy promotion package. High cost, high risk, but possibly highly profitable.

Page 77 Practice question

TV campaign can include a high profile, quality set of adverts and can be run at specific times when particular kinds of audience are watching. Cheaper than national broadcasts, and can refer to local outlets. But costs could be high even just for local TV. The adverts may also miss out some important customers, namely those out of the area who are just passing through. There is probably a need for other kinds of advertising too.

⊕ Page 81

Claims for brilliant performance without supporting evidence, adverts which are in bad taste or offensive to different groups, e.g. using sexual innuendo, adverts which show bad or dangerous driving, adverts which deliberately knock other firms' products.

Page 81 Practice question

a) If the only basis for complaint is the faded colour, then the customer has no claim. If the T-shirt has other faults, then she can insist on her money back under the Sale and Supply of Goods Act.

b) He could offer to exchange the T-shirt for another, so trying to encourage the customer to come back again.

c) She could contact the local Trading Standards Office or Citizen's Advice Bureau.

d) They could help her take her case to a small claims court. They could also give publicity to any poor practice, which might deter others from using that business.

◎ Page 83

Potential costs might include: extra congestion and the need for new roads, pollution (exhaust fumes, noise), loss of jobs in local high street, loss of choice as new centres tend to have a limited range of well-known national chain stores.

Page 83 Practice question

1. Extra spending in local shops, extra jobs for local workers, new road schemes, new public transport services.

2. Traffic congestion and disruption while theme park is built, noise disturbance once it is open, reduction in customers for other nearby attractions, a loss of land which could have been used for other purposes.

3. The theme park owners might be asked to spend money on local improvement schemes as part of the original agreement. There might be a local or national tax collection to help pay for costs. Part of the entry prices paid by customers could be used to help fund local services.

Page 84 Practice question

1. Carco pay no tax on new buildings and pay lower rates than would otherwise apply.

2. They will have the active support of the local council and will be part of a brand new industrial estate with good facilities.

3. The region needs the jobs and the extra spending brought into the area. People need to feel hopeful for the future. The national economy benefits because investment by a foreign company is seen as a sign of confidence in the country, its workers and the government, and appears as a positive figure in the UK balance of payments.

Page 87 Practice question

1. There are no barriers to trade within the market. Customers can buy anywhere, businesses can sell anywhere, workers can work anywhere, without extra taxes.

2. The same rules apply throughout, so it is easier for businesses to sell in foreign countries within the market than in foreign countries outside. There are fewer delays and less paperwork for goods moving across national borders.

3. A foreign firm, such as a Japanese car company, knows that, once based in an EU country, it can trade with other members without any barriers. If the same company tried to sell cars from outside the EU, it would have to negotiate separate deals with each country.

◎ Page 89

1. no taxes on exports
2. government-supported trade fair
3. import quota

Page 89 Practice question

1a) Japanese visitors will be able to buy more for their money so trade should go up.

1b) Fewer visitors might be expected generally. She might have to postpone the extension of her restaurant.

2. If the government could manage the exchange rate in such a way that businesses knew the rate for the next few months/year, it would give businesses more confidence in taking risky decisions. Trade fairs abroad might also be used to promote businesses like Jo's.

Photograph credits

P8 Bread factory: © Tony Stone Images/Michael Rosenfeld
P8 Co-op: © Co-operative Retail Services
P8 Wheat farmer: © Tony Stone Images/Andy Sacks
P8 Local Bakery © Rex Features
P22 Trucks leaving the warehouse: © Pictor
P22 Printing Works: © Greenshires Printers
P22 Teletubbies book, © BBC Educational Publishing, with thanks to Teletubbies.
P36 Small Business Unit: © Robert Harding Picture Library
P66 Storytime and Poetry Corner 2 © BBC Educational Publishing; Other photographs by courtesy of Teletubbies Magazine and Learning is Fun Magazine.
P78 Computers on sale in store: © The Stock Market/ Jeff Zaruba
P78 PC World: © PC World
P78 Derelict factory: © Tony Stone Images/Andy Sacks
P78 Crates of computers on dock: © Rex Features
All other photographs: © BBC/John Jefford